The '60

.
:

If You Remember It You Didn't Live It.

Copyright 2013 Jeffrey R. Crimmel

Cover Design by Rita Toews

Prologue

Reading about the '60s may only seems relevant to a certain sector of the population old enough to have lived during this time. If you were 40 or more in the '60s, you probably were disgusted by events in America and are too old now to even care. Many in this age group are no longer experiencing life in human form. If you were too young you may have been told stories from this period from an older uncle, brother-in-law or some family friend. He or she probably said they were also at a certain rock concert in Woodstock, N.Y. in 1969. This last fact may or may not be true. I am making a guess but if all the people who said they went to that concert and actually did, the numbers of attendees would have been in the millions.

The '60s was an age of heightened awareness. Americans were forever changed in the way they thought about many things in their lives. Food, music, war, women's rights, drugs, government, civil rights, Cuba, sex and marriage, religion, clothing, education, sports, moon landing and the news media were just a few of those things that changed. Those of you who were involved in any of these issues, no matter what position you took, became a part of this transitional period. The conflict between those who supported the status quo and those who pushed for change made the '60s what it was. It also helped in the continuous transformation of what America is today. We are a country of opposing ideas and values with each faction holding onto their beliefs as if it were the only truth.

Exploring many of these topics and many of the events I observed while living during this period should allow the reader who participated in the '60s to reflect on their own experiences during this metamorphosis of life. I have used Wikipedia to give a more accurate description of the events and people mentioned throughout the book. I used this source because it is the only information bank that is constantly changing and adding to the content. The world is constantly changing and Wikipedia seems to have recognized this fact. It is constantly updating every topic with the latest data available from their own sources or from the many readers who have information to add.

For those who were too young to join in during this time period and want to know what the '60s was like, here is an opportunity. The parents of those who lived during this era are now having a new expression on another plane of existence and never liked long hair and rock music anyway. Even the ones who had a chance to become involved and chose not to do so by staying in the '50s with their white picket fence and two-car garage until disco arrived in the '70s, here is what you missed.

Chapters

Chapter One   **Food**

Chapter Two   **Music**

Chapter Three   **Drugs and College In The '60s**

Chapter Four   **A Police Action Called Vietnam**

Chapter One
Food

While growing up I lived in Fresno,
California for a year from 1956 to 1957. I
remembered this new hamburger restaurant
called Mc Donald's. The single McDonald's
burger restaurant in Fresno kept advertising
how many burgers they had sold on a big sign
on the front of the store. The first sign read,
"Over 500,000 sold". For the year that I lived
in Fresno the sign kept changing and the
number kept getting larger. I remember
saying,

"Wow, mom, look! They have now sold over
750,000 hamburgers. They must be good
burgers because look how many they have
sold."

The measure of how good something was
seemed to be in the quantity and not the
quality. So began the first of the many
different fast food chains and the shift of the
average diet in America from home cooked
food to something fried, wrapped and handed
to you through a window from a building to
you in your car. By the time I moved back to
San Diego and La Jolla the simple looking

little burger store with the golden arches had a sign that now read,

"Over 1.2 million sold".

In one year this chain of a few restaurants on the west coast had sold over 700,000 burgers. The next year when we returned to Fresno to visit our grandparents the sign read,

"Over 5 million sold"

In the year we were away from Fresno many more franchises were built in California and other states. The culture of American cuisine had changed forever.

Early History of McDonalds

In 1937, Patrick McDonald opened "The Airdrome" restaurant at the Monrovia Airport in Monrovia, California. Hamburgers were ten cents, and all-you-can-drink orange juice was five cents. In 1940 his two sons, Maurice and Richard, moved the entire building 40 miles to the corner of 14th and E Streets in San Bernardino, California. The restaurant was renamed "McDonald's".

In 1948, the brothers Richard and Maurice McDonald introduced the "Speeder Service System" which established the principles of the modern fast-food restaurant. In 1954, Ray Kroc, a seller of Multimixer milkshake machines, learned that brothers Richard and Maurice (Dick and Mac) McDonald were using eight of his high-tech Multimixers in their San Bernardino, California, restaurant. His curiosity was piqued, and he went to San Bernardino to take a look at the McDonalds' restaurant.

The McDonald Brothers had been in the restaurant business since 1937. In 1948, they closed down a successful carhop drive-in to establish the streamlined operation Ray Kroc saw in 1954. The menu was simple: hamburgers, cheeseburgers, french fries, shakes, soft drinks, and apple pie. The carhops were eliminated to make McDonald's a self-serve operation. Mac and Dick McDonald had taken great care in setting up their kitchen like an assembly line, to ensure maximum efficiency.

Believing that the McDonald formula was a ticket to success, Kroc suggested that they franchise their restaurants throughout the country. When they hesitated to take on this additional burden, Kroc volunteered to do it for them. He returned to his home outside of Chicago with rights to set up McDonald's restaurants throughout the country, except in a handful of territories in California and Arizona already licensed by the McDonald brothers. Kroc's first McDonald's restaurant opened in Des Plaines, Illinois, near Chicago, on April 15, 1955, the same day that Kroc incorporated his company as McDonald's Corporation.

Once the Des Plaines restaurant was operational, Kroc sought franchisees for his McDonald's chain. The first snag came quickly. In 1956 he discovered that the McDonald brothers had licensed the franchise rights for Cook County, Illinois to the Frejlack Ice Cream Company. Kroc was incensed that the McDonalds had not informed him of this arrangement. He purchased the rights back for $25,000, five times what the Frejlacks had originally paid and pressed forward. McDonald's grew slowly for its first three years. By 1958, there were 34 restaurants. In 1959, however, Kroc opened 67 new restaurants, bringing the total to 101 locations. **Wikipedia**

During the 60's many other burger chains started up and the competition for the quick all American meal on the run had begun.

Burger King and Wendy's were two other giants that compete on a national scale with the Golden arches. Bob's Big Boy had a few stores around but never made the giant franchise shift to make their product a fast food establishment. They preferred the 'sit down and eat a burger' approach. The double-decker was Bob's claim to fame.

History of Bob's Big Boy

In 1936, Bob Wian sold his prized DeSoto Roadster to purchase a small hamburger stand in Glendale, California. He named it Bob's Pantry.

One night in 1937, a regular customer requested something different for a change. Bob went to work and the first double-decker hamburger was born.

Customers couldn't get enough of Bob's new creation. One fan in particular was a chubby six-year-old boy in droopy overalls.

He would often help Bob sweep up in exchange for a free burger. In honor of his young friend, Wian decided to name the better burger the Big Boy. Another regular customer, a movie studio animator, sketched the now famous character on a napkin.
The rest is history.
Wikipedia

Mexican food chains like Taco Bell made their move to get ready-made rice and beans with a burrito handed to you in your car as you hurried off to work during your lunch break. By 2:00 p.m. everyone in the office knew where you were from 12:00 until 1:00 p.m. because Beano was not invented yet. The expression, 'Beans, beans the musical fruit, the more you eat, the more you toot,' became a popular expression.

History of Taco Bell

Taco Bell was founded by Glen Bell. He first opened a hot dog stand called Bell's Drive-In in San Bernardino, California in 1946 when he was 23 years old. Six years later, he sold the stand and opened a new one two years later, this time selling tacos under the name of Taco-Tia. Over the next few years Bell owned and operated a number of restaurants in southern California including four called El Taco. Bell sold the El Tacos to his partner and built the first Taco Bell in Downey in 1962. In 1962, he sold Taco-Tia. Kermit Becky, a former Los Angeles police officer, bought the first Taco Bell franchise from Glen Bell in 1964 (with a little encouragement from another L.A. police officer Joseph Charles Zeller), and located it in Torrance. The company grew rapidly, and by 1967, the 100th restaurant opened at 400 South Brookhurst in Anaheim. In 1970, Taco Bell went public with 325 restaurants. In 1978, PepsiCo purchased Taco Bell from Glen Bell. **Wikipedia**

My work experience with fast food burgers came in 1962 when I was hired at a Swedish owned burger joint in Pacific Beach, California called Swendson's Burgers. His sandwich consisted of two buns, a meat patty and a little sauce on the meat. One burger cost 19 cents but if you bought five of them the price was a dollar. Either Swendson never did the math or he was smart enough to realize the general American public did not know how to multiple 5 times 19. If they did then the correct price for five burgers should have been 95 cents. Only one or two people ever brought up this discrepancy during the time I worked for the Swede. Maybe the un-accountable extra nickel was a clue that the education system in America was slipping, even in the year 1962.

Healthy alternatives in the food industry were also appearing during this period in our history. Stores and restaurants, serving food not sprayed by DDT and other insecticides used to kill bugs, became popular. One such store opened in Isla Vista near the University of California at Santa Barbara and many of the hippies who started to attend college worked in these establishments providing whole wheat, sugar free, non-dairy alternatives to eating and drinking. The idea spread and soon the medical industry was exposing the DDT industry to society and telling the world this spray was not good for your health. Duh!

Rachel Carson wrote Silent Spring in 1962 suggesting the possibility of cancer being related to the use of these chemicals used for spraying food sources.

Silent Spring is a book written by Rachel Carson and published by Houghton Mifflin on 27 September 1962. The book is widely credited with helping launch the environmental movement.

The New Yorker started serializing *Silent Spring* in June 1962, and it was published in book form (with illustrations by Lois and Louis Darling) by Houghton Mifflin later that year. When the book *Silent Spring* was published, Rachel Carson was already a well-known writer on natural history, but had not previously been a social critic. The book was widely read—especially after its selection by the Book-of-the-Month Club and the *New York Times* best-seller list—and inspired widespread public concerns with pesticides and pollution of the environment. *Silent Spring* facilitated the ban of the pesticide DDT in 1972 in the United States.

The book documented detrimental effects of pesticides on the environment, particularly on birds. Carson accused the chemical industry of spreading disinformation, and public officials of accepting industry claims uncritically.

Silent Spring has been featured in many lists of the best nonfiction books of the twentieth century. In the Modern Library List of Best 20th-Century Nonfiction it was at #5, and it was at No.78 in the conservative *National Review*. Most recently, *Silent Spring* was named one of the 25 greatest science books of all time by the editors of *Discover Magazine*. **Wikipedia**

DDT (from its trivial name, **d**ichloro**d**iphenyl**t**richloroethane) is one of the most well-known synthetic insecticides. It is a chemical with a long, unique, and controversial history.

First synthesized in 1874, DDT's insecticidal properties were not discovered until 1939, and it was used with great success in the second half of World War II to control malaria and typhus among civilians and troops. The Swiss chemist Paul Hermann Müller was awarded the Nobel Prize in Physiology or Medicine in 1948 "for his discovery of the high efficiency of DDT as a contact poison against several arthropods." After the war, DDT was made available for use as an agricultural insecticide, and soon its production and use skyrocketed.

In 1962, *Silent Spring* by American biologist Rachel Carson was published. The book catalogued the environmental impacts of the indiscriminate spraying of DDT in the US and questioned the logic of releasing large amounts of chemicals into the environment without fully understanding their effects on ecology or human health. The book suggested that DDT and other pesticides may cause cancer and that their agricultural use was a threat to wildlife, particularly birds. Its publication was one of the signature events in the birth of the environmental movement, and resulted in a large public outcry that eventually led to DDT being banned in the US in 1972. DDT was subsequently banned for agricultural use worldwide under the Stockholm Convention, but its limited use in disease vector control continues to this day and remains controversial.

Along with the passage of the Endangered Species Act, the US ban on DDT is cited by scientists as a major factor in the comeback of the bald eagle, the national bird of the United States, from near-extinction in the contiguous US. **Wikipedia**

I have also included a history of health food and how far it has come today. America is still in a war between the fast food industry and those who support eating a healthy diet. From the looks of so many Americans in the middle sections of their bodies, the battles are still waging.

A whole new industry has developed which sells all the weight loss products and programs for Americans. Not much is mentioned in this new multi-million dollar industry that really speaks out against the poor eating habits of those wanting to lose weight. Several companies like Jenny Craig have their own food items, which the consumer buys and eats. For many overweight people the costs are beyond their ability to pay and a Big Mac is only $1.99. Guess who wins that one.

Speaking from the present as I write this book, the only advertisements I have seen, which addresses a change in eating for America has come from the first lady, Michelle Obama. The commercials do not attack any fast food products but instead gives the watcher a choice.

"It may be difficult to say no to your child who wants a sweet snack after school but it would be more difficult to be told your child has type 2 diabetes." (TV commercial)

For the past three years Mrs. Obama has grown foods in the White House vegetable garden and served these healthy products at the dining table for the president and their family. Her message is healthy eating and exercise. No expensive eating programs only the upper middle class or rich can afford. No fast foods, which may be cheap but lead the way to clogged arteries and a burden on the medical industry as they treat you with drugs and other alternatives to keep you alive. She pushes only healthy eating and natural food.

Health Food

The term *health food* has been used since the 1920's to refer to specific food claiming to be especially beneficial to health, although the term has no official definition. Some terms that are associated with health food are macrobiotics, natural foods, organic foods and whole foods. Macrobiotics is a diet focusing primarily on whole cereals. Whole cereals, along with other *whole foods*, are foods that are minimally processed. Whole cereals have their fiber, germ and hull intact and are considered more nutritious. Natural foods are simply foods that contain no artificial ingredients. Organic foods are foods that are grown without the use of conventional and artificial pesticides and must meet certain organic standards.

History of Health Food Stores

Whole Foods Market has brought large, multi-national corporate buying power to the health food store industry.

Many foods, which are now commonplace in groceries, first entered the market in the late 19th and early 20th centuries. Efforts by early health pioneers such as Sylvester Graham, Horace Greeley, John Harvey Kellogg, George Ohsawa, Ellen White and others spurred an interest in health food. As early as the 1920's and 1930's health food stores started opening in the United States and the United Kingdom selling products such as blackstrap molasses and brewer's yeast.

Perhaps the oldest health food store was founded by Thomas Martindale in 1869 as "Thomas Martindale Company" in Olde City Philadelphia. The Martindale family eventually moved the store to 10th and Filbert St. in the late 1930's and was heavily influenced by the new interest in health and wellness. The store manufactured their own coffee substitute made from dried figs called "Figco". Healthy foods were sold in the lunchroom, with all baked goods being sweetened with honey or maple syrup. Eventually the store evolved into what is known as Martindale's Natural Market which is still in existence today.

In 1896 a new building was built in Birmingham, England to house James Henry Cook's vegetarian restaurant, one of the first in England. In 1898, 'The Pitman Vegetarian Hotel', named after the famous vegetarian Sir Isaac Pitman, opened on the same site, and the proprietors subsequently opened a long-running health food store.

Frank A. Sawall, who earlier worked with John Harvey Kellogg, began selling powdered mineral drinks door to door and lecturing around the United States on the benefits of vitamin and mineral supplements, before opening Sawall Health Food Products, Inc, in 1936, the United States' oldest family-owned natural foods store still in existence today. It began with powdered minerals and vitamins and also sold natural and organic foods. Frank A. Sawall, a biochemist, was described as "America's Outstanding Health Teacher and Nationally known Nutritionist" in newspapers across the United States. He lectured extensively across the Midwest and the East Coast. Frank A. Sawall, expanded his stores in Michigan, including Detroit, Kalamazoo, Bay City, Grand Rapids, and Lansing, creating the first health foods store chain in the United States. Sawall Health Foods is now in it's fourth generation with Sawall's running the business.

The Proxmire Vitamin Bill of 1976 that kept the FDA from defining food supplements as "drugs" was hailed as a great achivement in the health foods industry at the time. Senator William Proxmire was married to Ellen Hodges Sawall.

The New Westminster store operated by Health Food Research, opened in 1954 on the outskirts of Vancouver, British Columbia. It was founded by Ella Birzneck, and modeled partly upon Russian "doctors' shops", which carried medicines, herbs, and special foods.

Health food stores became much more common in the 1960's in connection with the newly emerging ecology movement and counterculture.

Many health food stores are worker owned cooperatives and consumers' cooperatives due in part to the ability of cooperative buying power to bring lower costs to the consumer and their growth of popularity during the counterculture movement of the 1960's and 1970's.

Over the last decade, health food, and especially organic food, has entered the mainstream. Companies such as Whole Foods Market, a large multinational corporation,

have profited greatly and grown substantially during this expansion.
Wikipedia

Chapter Two
Music

The chapter about music in the 60's could become an encyclopedia of research and work. I am retired and have no intention of putting music under the microscope and writing a James Michener in depth coverage of the subject. I will leave that project up to those who lived and worked in this industry during their time spent in the music world. We all had our favorite groups during this period in history and for many of us music got us through to the 70s and beyond.

James Albert Michener (February 3, 1907 – October 16, 1997) was an American author of more than 40 titles, the majority of which were sweeping sagas, covering the lives of many generations in particular geographic locales and incorporating historical facts into the stories. Michener was known for the meticulous research behind his work.

Michener's major books include *Tales of the South Pacific* (for which he won the Pulitzer Prize for Fiction in 1948), *Hawaii, The Drifters, Centennial, The Source, The Fires of Spring, Chesapeake, Caribbean, Caravans, Alaska, Texas,* and *Poland.* His nonfiction works include the 1968 *Iberia* about his travels in Spain and Portugal, his 1992 memoir *The World Is My Home,* and *Sports in America. Return to Paradise* combines fictional short stories with Michener's factual descriptions the Pacific areas where they take place.
Wikipedia

Rock and roll has been overshadowed by the next generation's claim on the world of music. Heavy Metal, Rap, and Hip Hop are just a few that come to mind.

I cannot get too excited about the music today any more than my parent's generation could with Rock and Roll. Music is a generational thing and there is nothing worse than seeing a Rock and Roll older person trying to remain cool dressing in the clothing worn by their kids and attempting to fit into this era of music. A 50 year old wearing skinny jeans and a tank top is not a pretty sight. I still wear

Levi 501 blue jean and tee shirts and I will until, "The day the music dies, and I'll be singing bye, bye Miss American Pie."

American Pie is my all time best song to come out of this era plus just about anything the Beatles did. I feel I raised my kids right in regards to music. They have their own style of songs today but they also love the '60s and '70s music that I exposed them to. This era is one of those good things America and England did right and they did it together.

"**American Pie**" is a folk rock song by singer-songwriter Don McLean.

Recorded and released on the *American Pie* album in 1971, the single was a number-one U.S. hit for four weeks in 1972. A re-release in 1991 did not chart in the U.S., but reached number 12 in the UK. The song is a recounting of "The Day the Music Died" — the 1959 plane crash that killed Buddy Holly, Ritchie Valens and The Big Bopper (Jiles Perry Richardson, Jr.). The importance of "American Pie" to America's musical and cultural heritage was recognized by the Songs of the Century education project, which listed the song as the number five song of the twentieth century. Some Top 40 stations initially played only side two of the single, but the song's popularity eventually forced stations to play the entire piece. "American Pie" is Don McLean's signature song. **Wikipedia**

While we are still on the subject of music and reflecting onto the past I have to pass on my thoughts of the most talented singer and writer of music to come from the late '60s and continue on into the '70s and '80s. He is also the most controversial entertainer of all time. That, of course, is Michael Jackson. There are books written about him from people who knew him well and loved him and books from people that did not know him at all and ripped him and all that he stood for. My answer for those who had issues with Michael is to play his song, "Man in the Mirror." This song has a message for the world based on the ideas behind the Christian religion and the message from Jesus.

"Judge not lest ye be judged."

Michael's version of that message,

"If you want to make the world a better place, take a look at yourself and make a change."

We, as individuals, who want to change the world have to change how we see the world first. By judging others and what they believe in while thinking our way is the only path and lifestyle the world should follow, is far from the message of either men. Jesus and Michael were different but they both carried the same directive. Don't judge others but instead make the change within yourself in order to see the world as a better place to be.

For you readers who may try to interpret what I have said into the idea that Jesus and Michael are the same, the answer would be no. Michael was a gifted songwriter and I believe he used the teachings of Jesus in this song. That is all.

Man in the Mirror is a song by Michael Jackson. It peaked at number one in the United States when released as a single in early 1988 off his seventh solo album, *Bad*. It is one of Jackson's most critically acclaimed songs and it was nominated for Record of the Year at the Grammy Awards. The song topped the *Billboard* Hot 100 for two weeks.

The song peaked at number 8 in the UK Singles Charts in 1988, but in 2009, following the news of Jackson's death, the song peaked at number two, behind Cascada's "Evacuate the Dancefloor," having re-entered the chart at 11 the previous week.
Wikipedia

While Michael really belonged to the later years of music, he and his brothers were getting their start as the Jackson Five in the mid '60s and gained recognition more in the '70s. By 1980 Michael was performing on his own and the world declared him the King of Pop Music. He will, for me, go down in history as a complicated genius who brought dance into the music culture. His message to the world was not recognized fully because the press chose to focus on his controversial lifestyle and not his gift. Many people, including myself, connected with his love for the world in nature and his attempt to draw attention to its' preservation. He seemed to be a man searching for his lost childhood and expressing his love through what he knew. Music. I miss you Michael.

The Jackson 5 (also spelled *The Jackson Five*, or *The Jackson 5ive*), later known as

The Jacksons, (or simply **Jackson**) were an American popular music family group from Gary, Indiana.

Founding group members Jackie, Tito, Jermaine, Marlon and Michael formed the group after performing in an early incarnation called **The Jackson Brothers**, which originally consisted of a trio of the three older brothers. Active from 1964 to 1990, the Jacksons played from a repertoire of R&B, soul, pop and later disco. During their six-and-a-half-year Motown tenure, The Jackson 5 were one of the biggest pop-music phenomena of the 1970's, and the band served as the launching pad for the solo careers of their lead singers Jermaine and Michael, the latter brother later transforming his early Motown solo fame into greater success as an adult artist.

The Jackson 5 were one of very few in recording history to have their first four major label singles ("I Want You Back", "ABC", "The Love You Save", and "I'll Be There") reach the top of the *Billboard* Hot 100. Several later singles, among them "Mama's Pearl", "Never Can Say Goodbye" and "Dancing Machine", were Top 5 pop hits and number-one hits on the R&B singles chart. Most of the early hits were written and produced by a specialized songwriting team known as "The Corporation"; later Jackson 5 hits were crafted chiefly by Hal Davis, while early Jacksons hits were compiled by the team of Gamble and Huff before The Jacksons began writing and producing themselves in the late 1970's.

Significantly, they were one of the first black teen idols to appeal equally to white audiences, thanks partially to the successful promotional relations skills of Motown Records CEO Berry Gordy. With their departure from Motown to CBS in 1976, The Jacksons were forced to change their name and Jermaine was replaced with younger brother Randy as Jermaine chose to stay at Motown. During these years, they continued to have a number of hits such as "Enjoy Yourself", "Shake Your Body (Down to the Ground)", "Show You the Way to Go", and "Blame It on the Boogie".

After two years under the Philadelphia International Records label, they signed with Epic Records and asserted control of their songwriting, production, and image, and their success continued into the 1980s with hits such as "Can You Feel It", "This Place Hotel", "Lovely One", and "State of Shock". Their 1989 album *2300 Jackson Street* was recorded without Michael and Marlon, although they did appear on the title track. The disappointing sales of the album led to the group being dropped by their record label at the end of the year. The group has never formally broken up, but has been dormant since then, although all six brothers performed together at two Michael Jackson tribute concerts in September 2001.

Wikipedia

A third great artist and songwriter from the era of the 60's is John Lennon. Music was the media used to get a message through to people and both Michael and John along with the other Beatle songwriters like Paul McCartney used this avenue to its' fullest potential. Those who followed John and Paul, experimented with drugs, meditated, changed how they viewed the world and still came out of this period in one piece. We should look back and thank those who influenced us for the life-changing trip we took along with them. Those who were not into the music of this period and played Frank

Sinatra songs until Disco arrived in the '70s, there is little to be said other than that you missed some of the greatest sounds of this century.

John Winston Lennon, MBE (9 October 1940 – 8 December 1980) was an English musician and singer-songwriter who rose to worldwide fame as one of the founding members of The Beatles, one of the most commercially successful and critically acclaimed acts in the history of popular music. Along with fellow Beatle Paul McCartney, he formed one of the most successful songwriting partnerships of the 20th century.

Born and raised in Liverpool, Lennon became involved as a teenager in the skiffle craze; his first band, The Quarrymen, evolved into The Beatles in 1960. As the group disintegrated towards the end of the decade, Lennon embarked on a solo career that produced the critically acclaimed albums *John Lennon/Plastic Ono Band* and *Imagine*, and iconic songs such as "Give Peace a Chance" and "Imagine".

After his marriage to Yoko Ono in 1969, he changed his name to John Ono Lennon. Lennon disengaged himself from the music business in 1975 to devote time to his infant son Sean, but re-emerged in 1980 with a new album, *Double Fantasy*. He was murdered three weeks after its release.

Lennon revealed a rebellious nature and acerbic wit in his music, his writing, his drawings, on film, and in interviews, becoming controversial through his political and peace activism. He moved to New York City in 1971, where his criticism of the Vietnam War resulted in a lengthy attempt by Richard Nixon's administration to deport him, while some of his songs were adopted as anthems by the anti-war movement.

As of 2010, Lennon's solo album sales in the United States exceed 14 million units, and as writer, co-writer or performer, he is responsible for 25 number-one singles on the US Hot 100 chart. In 2002, a BBC poll on the 100 Greatest Britons voted him eighth, and in 2008, *Rolling Stone* ranked him the fifth-greatest singer of all-time. He was posthumously inducted into the Songwriters

Hall of Fame in 1987 and into the Rock and Roll Hall of Fame in 1994.
Wikipedia

Wikipedia

"Imagine" by John Lennon may be one song that carries over to the next generations. The message is simple. You start with your mind where all great ideas are born and hold onto the vision of a world without war, boundaries, famine and all the things seen as detrimental to mankind. Keep seeing the world in your mind as perfect without the above mentioned conditions and someday you may make the shift in your beliefs that such a world is possible, right here and now.

"Someday you may join us, and the world may be as one."

Besides John I do have to include the other three members, who influenced me the most during this period. The Beatles were followed in their lives and music by many in the US as well as Europe. In England the youth were divided between the skinheads who liked the message of the Rolling Stones and the youth who loved the Beatles. Fights in schools even broke out over who had the best music. The music of the Stones continues today and it is the longest-lived band in the history of music. For me the music of the Beatles spoke to my middle class upbringing in California. Becoming a skinhead was not in my life's plan even though I did like many Stone's songs.

The Beatles were an English rock band, active throughout the 1960's and were one of the most commercially successful and critically acclaimed acts in the history of popular music. Formed in Liverpool, by late 1962 the group consisted of John Lennon (rhythm guitar, vocals), Paul McCartney (bass guitar, vocals), George Harrison (lead guitar, vocals) and Ringo Starr (drums, vocals). Rooted in skiffle and 1950's rock and roll, the group later worked in many genres ranging from pop ballads to psychedelic rock, often incorporating classical and other elements in innovative ways. The nature of their enormous popularity, which first emerged as "Beatlemania", transformed as their songwriting grew in sophistication. They came to be perceived as the embodiment of ideals of the social and cultural revolutions of the 1960's.

Initially a five-piece line-up of Lennon, McCartney, Harrison, Stuart Sutcliffe (bass) and Pete Best (drums), they built their reputation playing clubs in Liverpool and Hamburg over a three-year period from 1960. Sutcliffe left the group in 1961, and Best was replaced by Starr the following year. Molded into a professional act by manager Brian Epstein, their musical potential was enhanced by the creativity of producer George Martin. They gained popularity in the United Kingdom after their first single, "Love Me Do", became a modest hit in late 1962, and acquired the nickname the "Fab Four" as Beatlemania grew in Britain over the following year.

By early 1964 they had become international stars, leading the "British Invasion" of the United States pop market. The band toured extensively around the world until August 1966, when they performed their final commercial concert. From 1966 they produced what many critics consider to be some of their finest material, including the innovative and widely influential albums *Revolver* (1966), *Sgt. Pepper's Lonely Hearts Club Band* (1967), *The Beatles* (1968) and *Abbey Road* (1969). After their break-up in 1970, the ex-Beatles each found success in individual musical careers.

Lennon was murdered outside his home in New York City in 1980, and Harrison died in Los Angeles of cancer in 2001. McCartney and Starr remain active.

The Beatles are the best-selling band in history, and over four decades after their break-up, their recordings are still in demand. They have had more number one albums on the UK charts and have held the top spot longer than any other musical act. According to the RIAA, they have sold more albums in the United States than any other artist, and they topped *Billboard* magazine's list of all-time Hot 100 artists in 2008. They have received 7 Grammy Awards from the American National Academy of Recording

Arts and Sciences and 15 Ivor Novello Awards from the British Academy of Songwriters, Composers and Authors. They were collectively included in *Time* magazine's compilation of the 20th century's 100 most influential people.

Wikipedia

The Beatles in 1964
Top: John Lennon, Paul McCartney
Bottom: George Harrison, Ringo Starr

Wikipedia

For you Stones lovers I have included the Wikipedia bio of this group as well. After all, they are still going after 50 years of playing music together.

The Rolling Stones are an English rock band, formed in London in April 1962 by Brian Jones (guitar, harmonica), Ian Stewart (piano), Mick Jagger (lead vocals, harmonica), and Keith Richards (guitar). Bassist Bill Wyman and drummer Charlie Watts completed the early line-up. The emergence of the Rolling Stones has been credited for the greater international popularity of the primitive urban blues typified by Chess Records' artists such as Muddy Waters, who wrote "Rollin' Stone", the song from which the band drew its name. Though R&B and blues cover songs dominated the Rolling Stones' early material, their repertoire has always included rock and roll. The Rolling Stones' endurance and relevance, critic and musicologist Robert Palmer said, is due to their being "rooted in traditional verities, in rhythm-and-blues and soul music" while "more ephemeral pop fashions have come and gone".

Jones led the band until Jagger and Richards assumed leadership after teaming as songwriters. In 1969 Jones' diminishing contributions to the band and his inability to tour, due to poor health and legal complications, caused him to leave the band three weeks before drowning in his swimming pool. Jones' replacement Mick Taylor stayed with the band until leaving voluntarily in 1974, with Ronnie Wood taking his place since then. Wyman retired from the band in 1993; his replacement Darryl Jones has not been made a full member. Stewart was taken from the official line-up in 1963 and continued as the band's road manager and occasional pianist until his death in 1985. Since 1982, Chuck Leavell has been the band's primary keyboardist.

First popular in Europe, the Rolling Stones quickly became successful in North America during the British Invasion of the mid 1960s. Having released 22 studio albums in the United Kingdom (24 in the United States), nine live albums (ten in the US), and numerous compilations, their worldwide sales are estimated at more than 200 million albums. *Sticky Fingers* (1971) began a string of eight consecutive studio albums reaching number one in the United States. Their most recent album of entirely new material, *A Bigger Bang*, was released in 2005. In 1989, the Rolling Stones were inducted into the Rock and Roll Hall of Fame, and in 2004, they ranked number 4 in *Rolling Stone* magazine's 100 Greatest Artists of All Time. In 2008, *Billboard* magazine ranked the Rolling Stones at number ten on "The Billboard Hot 100 Top All-Time Artists". **Wikipedia**

The Rolling Stones

Wikipedia

A **skinhead** is a member of a subculture that originated among working class youths in London, England in the 1960s and then soon spread to other parts of the United Kingdom, and later to other countries around the world. Named for their close-cropped or shaven heads, the first skinheads were greatly

influenced by West Indian (specifically Jamaican) rude boys and British mods, in terms of fashion, music and lifestyle. Originally, the skinhead subculture was primarily based on those elements, not politics or race. Since then, however, attitudes toward race and politics have become factors by which some skinheads align themselves. The political spectrum within the skinhead scene ranges from the far right to the far left, although many skinheads are apolitical. Fashion-wise, skinheads range from a clean-cut 1960s mod-influenced style to less-strict punk- and hardcore-influenced styles.
Wikipedia

Music was huge during the '60s and there were many changes that came along within the rock and roll era. Each generation gave their twist on music so the media would have something to write about. Elvis began swinging his hips on the Ed Sullivan show in the 50s. The children screamed their approval and parents verbalized their disgust.

"That man is a heathen and will rot in hell for displaying such vulgarity."

As the Beach Blanket movies along with the Mickey Mouse club and 'Locomotion' made way for the more controversial groups like the Jefferson Airplane and 'White Rabbit', a generation of listeners asked the question,

"What pill will make you larger and which one will make you small? The ones that my mother gives me do not do anything at all except relieve my headache."

Jefferson Airplane was an American rock band formed in San Francisco in 1965. A pioneer of the psychedelic rock movement, Jefferson Airplane was the first band from the San Francisco scene to achieve mainstream commercial and critical success.

The band performed at the three most famous American rock festivals of the 1960s—Monterey (1967), Woodstock (1969) and Altamont (1969)—as well as headlining the first Isle of Wight Festival. Their recordings were internationally successful, and they scored two US Top 10 hit singles and a string of Top 20 albums. Their 1967 record *Surrealistic Pillow* is regarded as one of the key recordings of the so-called Summer of Love and brought the group international recognition. Two chart hits from the album, "Somebody to Love" and "White Rabbit", are listed in *Rolling Stone's* "500 Greatest Songs of All Time".

Successor bands to Jefferson Airplane include Jefferson Starship and Starship; spinoffs include Hot Tuna and KBC Band. Jefferson Airplane was inducted into the Rock and Roll Hall of Fame in 1996.

White Rabbit
------Jefferson Airplane

One pill makes you larger
And one pill makes you small
And the ones that mother gives you
Don't do anything at all
Go ask Alice
When she's ten feet tall

And if you go chasing rabbits
And you know you're going to fall
Tell 'em a hookah smoking caterpillar
Has given you the call
Call Alice
When she was just small

When men on the chessboard

Get up and tell you where to go
And you've just had some kind of mushroom
And your mind is moving slow
Go ask Alice
I think she'll know

When logic and proportion
Have fallen sloppy dead
And the White Knight is talking backwards
And the Red Queen's "off with her head!"
Remember what the dormouse said;
"Keep YOUR HEAD

_____

Keep your head"

Wikipedia

For me, White Rabbit was one of the best
songs describing the psychedelic period of the
'60s. It seemed to cover what a lot of the
youth and young adults were doing as they
explored the regions of their mind unclouded
by alcohol and other substances of their
parents generation. "Valley of the Dolls"
described what life could be like under the
influence of pills and booze.

Valley of the Dolls was an instant success
when it was first published. Since then it has

sold more than 30 million copies. As the first roman à clef by a female author to achieve this level of sales in America, it led the way for other authors such as Jackie Collins to depict the private lives of the real-life rich and famous under a veneer of fiction. ***Valley of the Dolls*** is a novel by American writer Jacqueline Susann, published in 1966. The "dolls" within the title is a slang term for downers, barbiturates used as sleep aids. **Wikipedia**

Rock groups and music in the '60s became caught up in drugs. Some music people handled the fame and glory while others crashed and burned. "Expand you mind" became a catch phrase and the use of marijuana in the '60s became one with this form of entertainment.

The music in the 60's came to a head when the concert called 'Woodstock' in the state of New York materialized. Movies have been written about it. People I met while traveling in India said they were there and just about everyone who was old enough to listen to the music of the era knew where they were in the 'summer of love.'

Woodstock

Woodstock Music & Art Fair (informally, **Woodstock** or **The Woodstock Festival**) was a music festival, billed as "An Aquarian Exposition: 3 Days of Peace & Music". It was held at Max Yasgur's 600-acre dairy farm in the Catskills near the hamlet of White Lake in the town of Bethel, New York, from August 15 to August 18, 1969. Bethel, in Sullivan County, is 43 miles (69 km) southwest of the town of Woodstock, New York, in adjoining Ulster County.

During the rainy weekend, thirty-two acts performed outdoors in front of 500,000 concert-goers. It is widely regarded as a pivotal moment in popular music history. *Rolling Stone* called it one of the *50 Moments That Changed the History of Rock and Roll*.

The event was captured in the 1970 documentary movie *Woodstock*, an accompanying soundtrack album, and Joni Mitchell's song "Woodstock" which commemorated the event and became a major hit for Crosby, Stills, Nash & Young.

Woodstock was initiated through the efforts of Michael Lang, John Roberts, Joel Rosenman, and Artie Kornfeld. It was Roberts and Rosenman who had the finances. Lang had experience as a promoter and had already organized the largest festival on the East Coast at the time, the Miami Pop Festival, which had an estimated 100,000 people attend the two day event. Roberts and Rosenman placed the following advertisement in *The New York Times* and *The Wall Street Journal* under the name of Challenge International, Ltd.:

"Young men with unlimited capital looking for interesting, legitimate investment opportunities and business propositions".

Lang and Kornfeld noticed the ad, and the four men got together originally to discuss a retreat-like recording studio in Woodstock, but the idea evolved into an outdoor music and arts festival, although even that was initially envisioned on a smaller scale, perhaps featuring some of the big name artists who lived in the Woodstock area (such as Bob Dylan and The Band). There were differences in approach among the four: Roberts was disciplined, and knew what was needed in order for the venture to succeed, while the laid-back Lang saw Woodstock as a new, relaxed way of bringing businesspeople together. There were further doubts over the venture, as Roberts wondered whether to consolidate his losses and pull the plug, or to continue pumping his own finances into the project.

In April 1969, newly-minted superstars Creedence Clearwater Revival were the first act to sign a contract for the event, agreeing to play for $10,000. The promoters had experienced difficulty landing big-name groups prior to Creedence committing to play. Creedence drummer Doug Clifford later commented "Once Creedence signed, everyone else jumped in line and all the other big acts came on." Given their 3:00 a.m. start time and non-inclusion (at Creedence frontman John Fogerty's insistence) in the *Woodstock* film, Creedence members have expressed bitterness over their experiences at the famed festival.

Woodstock was designed as a profit-making venture, aptly titled "Woodstock Ventures". It famously became a "free concert" only after it became obvious that the event was drawing hundreds of thousands more people than the organizers had prepared for. Tickets for the event cost $18 in advance (equivalent to $75 in 2009 after adjusting for inflation) and $24 at the gate for all three days. Ticket sales were limited to record stores in the greater New York City area, or by mail via a post office box at the Radio City Station Post Office located in Midtown Manhattan. Around 186,000 tickets were sold beforehand and organizers anticipated approximately 200,000 festival-goers would turn up.

Selection of the venue

The crowd and stage in 1969.

The concert was originally scheduled to take place in the 300-acre Mills Industrial Park (in the town of Wallkill, New York, which Woodstock Ventures had leased for $10,000 in the Spring of 1969. Town officials were assured that no more than 50,000 would attend. Town residents immediately opposed the project. In early July the Town Board passed a law requiring a permit for any gathering over 5,000 people. On July 15, 1969, the Wallkill Zoning Board of Appeals officially banned the concert on the basis that the planned portable toilets would not meet town code. Reports about the ban, however, turned out to be a publicity bonanza for the festival.

Max Yasgur's dairy farm in 1968.
According to Elliot Tiber in his 2007 book *Taking Woodstock*, Tiber offered to host the event on his 15 acres (61,000 m^2) motel grounds, and had a permit for such an event. He claims to have introduced the promoters to dairy farmer Max Yasgur. Lang, however, disputes Tiber's account, and says that Tiber introduced him to a real estate salesman, who

drove him to Yasgur's farm without Tiber. Sam Yasgur, Max's son, agrees with Lang's account. Yasgur's land formed a natural bowl sloping down to Filippini Pond on the land's north side. The stage would be set at the bottom of the hill with Filippini Pond forming a backdrop. The pond would become a popular skinny dipping destination.

The organizers once again told Bethel authorities they expected no more than 50,000 people.

Despite resident opposition and signs proclaiming, "Buy No Milk. Stop Max's Hippy Music Festival", Bethel Town Attorney Frederick W. V. Schadt and building inspector Donald Clark approved the permits, but the Bethel Town Board refused to issue them formally. Clark was ordered to post stop work orders.

Free concert
The late change in venue did not give the festival organizers enough time to prepare. At a meeting three days before the event, organizers felt they had two choices. One option was to improve the fencing and security, which might have resulted in violence; the other involved putting all their

resources into completing the stage, which would cause Woodstock Ventures to take a financial hit. The crowd, which was arriving in greater numbers and earlier than anticipated, made the decision for them. The fence was cut the night before the concert.

The festival

The influx of attendees to the rural concert site in Bethel created a massive traffic jam. Fearing chaos as thousands began descending on the community, Bethel did not enforce its codes. Eventually, announcements on radio stations as far away as WNEW-FM in Manhattan and descriptions of the traffic jams on television news programs discouraged people from setting off to the festival. Arlo Guthrie made an announcement that was included in the film saying that the New York State Thruway was closed. The director of the Woodstock museum discussed below said this never occurred. To add to the problems and difficulty in dealing with the large crowds, recent rains had caused muddy roads and fields. The facilities were not equipped to provide sanitation or first aid for the number of people attending; hundreds of thousands found themselves in a struggle against bad weather, food shortages, and poor sanitation.

On the morning of Sunday, August 17, New York Governor Nelson Rockefeller called festival organizer John Roberts and told him he was thinking of ordering 10,000 New York State National Guard troops to the festival. Roberts was successful in persuading Rockefeller not to do this. Sullivan County declared a state of emergency.

Although the festival was remarkably peaceful given the number of people and the conditions involved, there were two recorded fatalities: one from what was believed to be a heroin overdose and another caused in an accident when a tractor ran over an attendee sleeping in a nearby hayfield. There also were two births recorded at the event (one in a car caught in traffic and another in a hospital after an airlift by helicopter) and four miscarriages. Oral testimony in the film supports the overdose and run-over deaths and at least one birth, along with many logistical headaches.

Yet, in tune with the idealistic hopes of the 1960s, Woodstock satisfied most attendees.

There was a sense of social harmony, which, with the quality of music, and the overwhelming mass of people, many sporting bohemian dress, behavior, and attitudes helped to make it one of the enduring events of the century.

After the concert, Max Yasgur, who owned the site of the event, saw it as a victory of peace and love. He spoke of how nearly half a million people filled with possibilities of disaster, riot, looting, and catastrophe spent the three days with music and peace on their minds. He states that "if we join them, we can turn those adversities that are the problems of America today into a hope for a brighter and more peaceful future..."

Performing artists

Friday, August 15
- Richie Havens
- Swami Satchidananda – gave the invocation for the festival
- Sweetwater
- Bert Sommer
- Ravi Shankar
- Tim Hardin
- Melanie

- Arlo Guthrie
- Joan Baez
- **Saturday, August 16**
- Quill
- Country Joe McDonald
- John Sebastian
- Santana
- Keef Hartley Band
- The Incredible String Band
- Canned Heat
- Mountain
- Grateful Dead
- Creedence Clearwater Revival
- Janis Joplin with The Kozmic Blues Band[25]
- Sly & the Family Stone
- The Who
- Jefferson Airplane

Sunday, August 17 to Monday, August 18
- The Grease Band
- Joe Cocker
- Country Joe and the Fish
- Ten Years After
- The Band
- Blood, Sweat & Tears
- Johnny Winter featuring his brother, Edgar Winter
- Crosby, Stills, Nash & Young
- Paul Butterfield Blues Band

- Sha-Na-Na
- Jimi Hendrix

Wikipedia

I have ended the section on music in the 60's with Woodstock because it is still today the most memorable moment in the history of music where estimated 500,000 young people got together in a weekend of fun and music. I have seen several movies, which have tried to cover the event; but the best one so far for me has been 'Taking Woodstock' by Ang Lee.

Taking Woodstock is a 2009 American comedy-drama film about the Woodstock Festival of 1969, directed by Ang Lee. The screenplay by James Schamus is based on the memoir *Taking Woodstock: A True Story of a Riot, a Concert, and a Life* by Elliot Tiber and Tom Monte.

The film premiered at the 2009 Cannes Film Festival, and opened in New York and Los Angeles on August 26, 2009, before its wide theatrical release two days later.

Wikipedia

Those who were disgusted by the hippies of this era and the use of marijuana instead of alcohol as a social stimulant should think about this. Imagine 500,000 drunk rednecks coming together for a concert and having to put up with the conditions of the weekend. Violence and death would have been in high numbers and riots would have occurred. Alcohol has never been a stimulant representing the 60's. Booze is still today the number one cause of traffic deaths in America. It is also legal. Put that fact in your pipe and smoke it.

In all fairness to representing multiple sides of the music world, country western music had a response to Woodstock and the hippies of California. 'Okie from Muskogee' was their answer to the pot smoking, LSD dropping generation that was threatening their way of life of drinking longneck beers and 'white lightning.' Long hair was a threat to the cowboy mentality. Challenging things like war and government was not something rednecks did. Speaking out against the government was not the cowboy way.

This 'follow without thinking' way of existence allowed the army to recruit young men that never thought if they were doing the right thing. Not signing up to fight those

60

'damn communists' would be considered an act of treason in the state of Texas. Fighting was a way of life in cowboy country. Just go to a country western bar and see how many bouncers are needed to break up the fights that occur. The movie 'Roadhouse' is a good example portraying this lifestyle.

"Okie from Muskogee" is an American country music song performed by its co-writer, Merle Haggard. Released in September 1969, the song became one of the most famous of his career.

Haggard told *The Boot* that he wrote the song after he became disheartened watching Vietnam War protests and incorporated that emotion and viewpoint into song. Haggard says, "When I was in prison, I knew what it was like to have freedom taken away. Freedom is everything. During Vietnam, there were all kinds of protests. Here were these [servicemen] going over there and dying for a cause — we don't even know what it was really all about. And here are these young kids that were free, bitching about it. There's something wrong with that and with [disparaging] those poor guys." He states that he wrote the song to support the troops.

Critic Kurt Wolff wrote that Haggard always considered what became a redneck anthem to be a spoof, and that today fans — even the hippies that are derided in the lyrics — have taken a liking to the song and find humor in some of the lyrics. In fact, cover versions of the song have been recorded by such countercultural acts as the Grateful Dead, The Beach Boys and Phil Ochs.

Written by Haggard and Roy Edward Burris (drummer for Haggard's backing band, The Strangers) during the height of the Vietnam War, "Okie from Muskogee" grew from the two trading one-liners about small-town life, where conservative values were the norm and outsiders with ideals contrary to those ways were unwelcome. Here, the singer reflects on how proud he is to hail from Middle America, where its residents were patriotic, and didn't smoke marijuana, take LSD, wear beads and sandals, burn draft cards or challenge authority.

While viewed as a satire of small-town America and its reaction to the anti-war protests and counterculture seen in America's larger cities, Allmusic writer Bill Janovitz writes that the song also "convincingly (gives) voice to a proud, straight-laced truck-driver type. ... (In the end, he identifies with the narrator. He does not position the protagonist as angry, reactionary, or judgmental; it is more that the guy, a self-confessed 'square,' is confused by such changes and with a chuckle comes to the conclusion that he and his ilk have the right sort of life for themselves."

Session personnel were James Burton, Roy Nichols and Jerry Reed on guitar; Chuck Berghofer on bass, and Ron Tutt on drums. **Wikipedia**

Country western music has come a long way from those attitudes of the 60's and today many male singers have long hair and the music has shifted from, 'my dog died and my girlfriend left me' to more upbeat songs which may or may not talk about the social issues of being broke and driving down the road in an old pickup. I even like many of the country western singers and songs of today and for sure the women singing western songs are the best looking in the whole music world.

I do have to include one of the best-known country singers of the day. Johnny Cash and his signature song taped in Folsom Prison is the most sold album today. He sang about the conditions of prisoners, their treatment and the bad water they had to drink.

John R. "Johnny" Cash (February 26, 1932 – September 12, 2003), was an American singer-songwriter, actor, and author, who has been called one of the most influential musicians of the 20th century. Although he is primarily remembered as a country music icon, his songs and sound spanned many other genres including rockabilly and rock and roll—especially early in his career—as well as blues, folk, and gospel. This crossover appeal led to Cash being inducted in the Country Music Hall of Fame, the Rock and Roll Hall of Fame, and Gospel Music Hall of Fame.

Cash was known for his deep, distinctive bass-baritone voice; for the "boom-chicka-boom" sound of his Tennessee Three backing band; for his rebelliousness, coupled with an increasingly somber and humble demeanor; for providing free concerts inside prison walls; and for his dark performance clothing, which earned him the nickname "The Man in

Black". He traditionally started his concerts by saying, "Hello, I'm Johnny Cash." He usually followed it up with his standard "Folsom Prison Blues".

Much of Cash's music, especially that of his later career, echoed themes of sorrow, moral tribulation and redemption. His signature songs include "I Walk the Line", "Folsom Prison Blues", "Ring of Fire", "Get Rhythm" and "Man in Black". He also recorded humorous numbers, including "One Piece at a Time" and "A Boy Named Sue"; a duet with his future wife, June Carter, called "Jackson"; as well as railroad songs including "Hey, Porter" and "Rock Island Line". Late in his career, Cash covered songs by several rock artists, most notably "Hurt" by Nine Inch Nails.

Wikipedia

Dance should be mentioned quickly in this section of the book because it doesn't fit in the food section and I do not remember all the dances that became popular in the '60s. The Twist is really the only dance that most people who grew up in this time period remember and when one mentions Twist,

Chubby Checker is the singer who made it popular.

"The Twist" is a song that gave birth to the Twist dance craze. The song was written and originally released in 1959 by Hank Ballard and the Midnighters as a B-side (to "Teardrops on Your Letter") but his version was only a moderate 1960 hit, peaking at #28 on the *Billboard* Hot 100.[1] The song, and the dance the Twist, was popularized in 1960 when the song was covered by Chubby Checker. His single became a hit, reaching #1 on the Billboard Hot 100 on September 19, 1960 (one week) and then setting a record by being the only single to reach #1 in two different chart runs when it resurfaced and topped the chart again on January 13, 1962 (two weeks).

In 1988, "The Twist" became popular once again, due to a new recording of the song by The Fat Boys featuring Chubby Checker. **Wikipedia**

Chubby Checker (born **Ernest Evans**, October 3, 1941) is an American singer-songwriter. He is widely known for popularizing the twist dance style, with his

1960 hit cover of Hank Ballard's R&B hit "The Twist". In September 2008 "The Twist" topped Billboard's list of the most popular singles to have appeared in the Hot 100 since its debut in 1958.[1]

"The Twist" had previously peaked at #16 on the *Billboard* rhythm and blues chart, in the 1959 version recorded by its author, Hank Ballard, whose band The Midnighters first performed the dance on stage. Checker's "Twist", however, was a nationwide smash, aided by his many appearances on Dick Clark's American Bandstand, the Top 10 American Bandstand ranking of the song, and the teenagers on the show who enjoyed dancing the Twist. The song was so ubiquitous that Checker felt that his critics thought that he could only succeed with dance records typecasting him as a dance artist. Checker later lamented:
"...in a way, "The Twist" really ruined my life. I was on my way to becoming a big nightclub performer, and "The Twist" just wiped it out.. It got so out of proportion. No one ever believes I have talent."
—Chubby Checker
Wikipedia

Chapter Three
Drugs and College in the '60s

I can choose to write about drugs in the '60s by gathering all the stories I have heard or becoming more personal with my exposure to the drug culture. I have selected the latter to make it more personal. After high school I left the quaint village of La Jolla in San Diego County and lived in Salzburg, Austria for one year. Being away from my roots and family influences was a first step towards finding my own way in life. In high school I was not into the party mentality of getting drunk at Sally's parents house who were out of town that weekend. I made up for my lack of alcohol-induced behavior during my year abroad.

Salzburg (help·info) (Austro-Bavarian: *Såizburg*; literally: "Salt Castle") is the fourth-largest city in Austria and the capital city of the federal state of Salzburg.

Salzburg's "Old Town" (*Altstadt*) has internationally renowned baroque architecture and one of the best-preserved city centres north of the Alps. It was listed as a UNESCO

World Heritage Site in 1997. The city is noted for its Alpine setting.

Salzburg was the birthplace of 18th-century composer Wolfgang Amadeus Mozart. In the mid-20th century, the city was the setting for parts of the American musical and film *The Sound of Music*.

The capital city of the State of Salzburg (*Land Salzburg*), the city has three universities. It has a large population of students who add liveliness and energy to the area, and the universities provide culture to the community. **Wikipedia**

Drinking in Europe is legal at age 16. Because it is much more relaxed on the continent there are nowhere near the problems with youth drinking we face in the tightly controlled age limit of 21 in America. Today American kids travel to Mexico on Spring breaks and parents can now see their bare breasted daughters on the Sports channels in the early morning. 'Girls Gone Wild' must be a sport by now. Young ladies of 17 or 18 can even order the video of their wild college school breaks for all their relatives like grandma or Aunt Julie for Christmas.

The **Girls Gone Wild** franchise, created by Joe Francis, is a video series by the production company Mantra Films, Inc., which is headquartered in Santa Monica, California.

The first Girls Gone Wild (GGW) film was released in 1997. The films center around sexual activity and always conform to the same formula. GGW videos usually involve a camera crew patrolling an area frequented by young attractive women, such as a spring break or Mardi Gras, vacation resorts, or nightclubs. The crews search for attractive young women who agree to expose their bodies for the camera, in exchange for a Girls Gone Wild branded t-shirt, shorts, or cap. Usually the women are encouraged to strip by crowds of on looking young men. In addition, women kiss each other and expose their breasts, buttocks, and/or genitalia.

Sometimes the camera crew follows a group of young females back to the GGW tour bus, a hotel or other location, and tapes them engaging in additional sexual activities. The company claims to only film amateurs rather than professional porn stars. The camera crews are normally young attractive men, in order to encourage the women to perform, and they receive a bonus for filming particularly attractive women or women who have just turned 18. Francis appears as the host of some of the films. Nightclub promoters pay up to $10,000 a night to host GGW film crews as they ensure large crowds. **Wikipedia**

Upon my return to the states my mother arranged for me to work in a Christian Camp for families and youth groups. I believe she was attempting to exorcise the devil out of my body after spending a year in Salzburg and Europe. The best advice I received from some of the others who worked at the retreat, located at an elevation of 5,280 feet or one mile closer to heaven, was for me to reapply to the University of Santa Barbara where I had been accepted the year before instead of opting for San Diego State.

The UC system was a more difficult institution to get into. In 1964 the state college system remained for those students who did not apply themselves in high school and earn a 3.0 GPA or students who did not have the tuition needed for the University of California higher learning. The state colleges were affordable in the '60s and California made education attainable for anyone wanting to 'expand their mind' and learn more about the world they lived in.

UCSB
In the late 1960's and early 1970's UCSB became nationally known as a hotbed of anti-Vietnam War activity. A bombing at the school's faculty club in 1969 killed the caretaker, Dover Sharp. In the spring of 1970 multiple occasions of arson occurred, including a burning of the Bank of America branch building in the student community of Isla Vista, during which time one male student, Kevin Moran, was shot and killed by police. UCSB's anti-Vietnam activity impelled Governor Ronald Reagan to impose a curfew and order the National Guard to enforce it. Weapon-carrying guardsmen were a common sight on campus and in Isla Vista during this time.
Wikipedia

In September of 1964 I was dropped off at the UCSB campus. I had never visited the school. My only view of the grounds came from the brochures sent out to those who were accepted to attend the University. Because I applied late and was accepted the previous year, fifty other young men and I were housed in navy barracks located a short bike ride from classes and the dining halls. The campus had been built on an old naval-training base overlooking the Pacific Ocean on cliffs rising 20 feet from the sandy beaches below.

I was housed with two other young men, both named John, in the large barrack room at the end of the hall. The other rooms each housed two men. The plan the school had for us was to spend a semester in these buildings and then move us into the dorms for the second semester. We would replace those students who could not handle the freedom of being away from home. The school held a ranking as one of the top ten party schools in Playboy magazine.

While living in the military units I was talked into joining ROTC by one of my roommates who came from a military family. He said it was an easy A grade and all you needed to do was to learn how to shine your brass belt buckle and spit-shine the tips of your shoes. Little did I know, many of those who signed up would be sent to Vietnam within the next four years dodging bullets along with Forest Gump, Lieutenant Dan and Bubba. They might even get to hear Adrian Cronauer on the radio saying,

"Good Morning, Vietnam."

Adrian Cronauer (born September 8, 1938 in Pittsburgh, Pennsylvania) is a former United States Air Force sergeant and radio personality whose experiences as an innovative deejay in Vietnam inspired the 1987 film *Good Morning, Vietnam.*

Cronauer co-wrote the original story for the film *Good Morning, Vietnam,* which was based on his experiences as a Saigon-based deejay during the Vietnam War, where he served from 1965 to 1966. His program was known as the "Dawn Buster". A subsequent special program on National Public Radio about the role of the American Forces Vietnam Network -- AFVN -- (military radio and television) earned Cronauer a 1992 Ohio State Award and two 1991 Gold Medals from the New York Radio Festival.

Wikipedia

While living in the naval housing unit I had
my first exposure to the weed that would soon
become a part of college life in the '60s. Two
men who looked much older than the rest of
us wet behind the ears 18 and 19 year olds,
lived in the room directly across from mine.
One of the men could have passed for Alan
Ginsberg's brother sporting a full black beard
and long curly hair. Both men spent their
evening locked in their room with loud music
blaring from the latest rock group out of San
Francisco. Having been gone from the States
for a year I had not made the shift in music
from, 'It's My Party and I'll Cry if I Want
To', to the rock bands in the early '60s. I had
a lot of catching up to do.

Many times during the semester the dorm rep.
named Gordy, also living in the building and
keeping an eye on us young pups, had to
knock on the door of the duo from the Bay
Area and ask them to keep the music down.
Each time they open their door a cloud of
smoke poured into the hallway. Gordy knew
nothing about the difference between the
smell of grass from Mexico and Camel
cigarettes. Neither did any of the other

students in the building. We all knew it smelled differently than most tobacco sold in the stores. As long as they kept the music down Gordy left them alone.

I believe the two young men from San Francisco became causalities of the first semester for college students away from home for the first time. One third of all freshmen students were expected to flunk out or go on academic probation. I never saw either of the pot smokers on campus again.

The A in ROTC and the B in German I, combined with the Cs from History and English enabled me to limp along into the second semester of higher education. As predicted we were moved into the dorms on campus overlooking the Pacific Ocean. Surfboards were kept in many of the rooms and when the winter surf picked up, hanging ten on the picture perfect waves breaking around the point just below the dorms became the early morning and evening activities of the surfing population. I grew up surfing in La Jolla and loved the sport but no longer owned a board needed to continue this water recreation.

I made a few friends in the dorms who became involved in my life when I left the country in the '70s. One was named Rich and he was now a sophomore living in the dorms. Rich had learned to play the guitar from his freshman roommate, Robbie Krieger. Robbie did not return to UCSB in 1964. His band, The Doors, went on to fame and fortune until the death of the lead singer, Jim Morrison, in Paris, France. "Light My Fire" lives on with the '60s generation and retirement homes across the country still play music from that time period. Those who participated in the rock and roll portion of this era still sing along because we all know the words.

The Doors were an American rock band formed in 1965 in Los Angeles, California, with vocalist Jim Morrison, keyboardist Ray Manzarek, drummer John Densmore, and guitarist Robby Krieger. The band took its name from Aldous Huxley's book *The Doors of Perception*, the title of which was a reference to a William Blake quotation: "If the doors of perception were cleansed every thing would appear to man as it is, infinite." They were among the most controversial rock acts of the 1960s, due mostly to Morrison's wild, poetic lyrics and charismatic but unpredictable stage persona. After Morrison's death in 1971, the remaining members continued as a trio until finally disbanding in 1973.

Although The Doors' active career ended in 1973, their popularity has persisted. According to the RIAA, they have sold over 35 million albums in the US alone. The band has sold nearly 100 million albums worldwide. Ray Manzarek and Robby Krieger continue to tour as Manzarek-Krieger, performing Doors songs exclusively. They were the first American band to accumulate eight consecutive gold LPs. Three of the band's studio albums, *The Doors* (1967), *Strange Days* (1967), and *L.A. Woman* (1971), were featured in the *Rolling Stone* list of The 500 Greatest Albums of All Time, at positions 42, 407 and 362 respectively. In 1993, The Doors were inducted into the Rock and Roll Hall of Fame. **Wikipedia**

I have always been a talker and a social life interested me at the time. My roommate from first semester had pledged a fraternity and now lived in the Frat he joined during the first semester. I was persuaded to go around and visit the different fraternities during pledge week and noticed how each house seemed to contain a type of young man who looked and acted just like each other. If you looked like a male model with an ivy-league haircut, you joined this house. If you were on the road to becoming an alcoholic and drinking and partying your way through your college years, there was a fraternity for you. John Belushi and the movie 'Animal House' best describe the individuals seeking this brotherhood of friends.

National Lampoon's Animal House is a 1978 American comedy film directed by John Landis. The film was a direct spin-off from *National Lampoon* magazine. The plot is about a misfit group of fraternity members who challenge the administrators of their university.

The screenplay was adapted by Douglas Kenney, Chris Miller and Harold Ramis from stories that were written by Miller and published in *National Lampoon* magazine. The stories were based on Miller's experiences in the Alpha Delta Phi fraternity at Dartmouth College. Other influences on the film came from Ramis' experiences in the

Zeta Beta Tau fraternity at Washington University in St. Louis, and producer Ivan Reitman's experiences at Delta Upsilon at McMaster University in Hamilton, Ontario. Of the lead actors, only John Belushi was an established star, but even he had not yet appeared in a movie, having gained his notoriety mainly from his Saturday Night Live television appearances. Several cast members, including Karen Allen, Tom Hulce and Kevin Bacon, were just beginning their movie careers.

Upon its initial release, *Animal House* received generally mixed reviews from critics, but *Time* and Roger Ebert proclaimed it one of the year's best. Filmed for $2.7 million, it is one of the most profitable movies of all time. Since its initial release, *Animal House* has garnered an estimated return of more than $141 million in the form of videos and DVDs, not including merchandising.

The film, along with 1977's *Kentucky Fried Movie*, also directed by Landis, was largely responsible for defining and launching the gross-out genre of films, which became one of Hollywood's staple genres. In 2001, the

United States Library of Congress deemed *Animal House* "culturally significant" and selected it for preservation in the National Film Registry. This film was #1 on Bravo's 100 Funniest Movies. It was #36 on AFI's *100 Years... 100 Laughs* list of the 100 best American comedies. In 2008, *Empire* magazine selected *Animal House* as one of *The 500 Greatest Movies of All Time*. **Wikipedia**

The athletics had a place to be with other jocks. The nerds with GPAs of 3.5 or higher found common ground in a group of men and eventually religion created a fraternity based on being Jewish. I found a group of men who seemed to have a mixture of all the houses combined and did not have a stereotype of pledge they were seeking. My roommate, John, from the first semester, was in this group and I decided to expand my horizons by joining them in their attempt to mold young men into upstanding individuals, ready for society.

It was now 1965 and I was becoming socialized into a fraternity that started in the south after the civil war. Alcohol was the drug of choice and events like toga and theme parties seemed to fill the calendar as we attempted to meet and date the girls being trained for society in the sororities found throughout the campus. In the '60s many of these young women still used higher education as a means to finding an educated man with the potential for a good job and the ability to care for her as a husband. Gloria Steinem had not yet made her move in 1965 but 'women's lib' was just around the corner.

Outside the walls of higher learning, the music world was starting to get noticed. Vietnam was still a small military exercise somewhere in Southeast Asia. Men were being drafted after high school and began their training in America's attempt to stop the flood of communism from reaching our shores. The Beatles had arrived in New York and Ed Sullivan promised,

"A really big show."

The Ed Sullivan Show is an American TV variety show that originally ran on CBS from Sunday June 20, 1948 to Sunday June 6, 1971, and was hosted by New York entertainment columnist Ed Sullivan.

In 2002, *The Ed Sullivan Show* was ranked #15 on TV Guide's 50 Greatest TV Shows of All Time.

In late 1963, Sullivan and his entourage happened also to be passing through Heathrow and witnessed how The Beatles' fans greeted the group on their return from Stockholm, where they had performed a television show as warm-up band to local star Lill Babs. Sullivan was intrigued, telling his entourage it was the same thing as Elvis all over again. He initially offered Beatles manager Brian Epstein top dollar for a single show but the Beatles manager had a better idea—he wanted exposure for his clients: the Beatles would instead appear three times on the show, at bottom dollar, but receive top billing and two spots (opening and closing) on each show.

The Beatles appeared on three consecutive Sundays in February 1964 to great anticipation and fanfare as "I Want to Hold Your Hand" had swiftly risen to No. 1 in the charts. Their first appearance on February 9 is considered a milestone in American pop culture and the beginning of the British Invasion in music. The broadcast drew an estimated 73 million viewers, at the time a record for US television, and was characterized by an audience composed largely of screaming hysterical teenage girls in tears.

The Beatles followed Ed's show opening intro, performing "All My Loving", "Till There Was You" which featured the names of the group members superimposed on close up shots, including the famous "Sorry girls, he's married" caption on John Lennon, and "She Loves You". They returned later in the program to perform "I Saw Her Standing There" and "I Want to Hold Your Hand."

The following week's show was broadcast from Miami Beach where Muhammad Ali (then Cassius Clay) was in training for his first title bout with Sonny Liston. The occasion was used by both camps for publicity. On the evening of the television show (February 16) a crush of people nearly prevented the band from making it onstage. A wedge of policemen were needed and the band began playing "She Loves You" only seconds after reaching their instruments. They continued with "This Boy", and "All My Loving" and returned later to close the show with "I Saw Her Standing There" and "I Want to Hold Your Hand."

They were shown on tape February 23 (this appearance had been taped earlier in the day on February 9 before their first live appearance). They followed Ed's intro with "Twist and Shout" and "Please Please Me" and closed the show once again with "I Want to Hold Your Hand."

The Beatles appeared live for the final time on August 14, 1965. The show was broadcast September 12, 1965 and earned Sullivan a 60 percent share of the nighttime audience for one of the appearances. This time they followed three acts before coming out to perform "I Feel Fine", "I'm Down", and "Act Naturally" and then closed the show with "Ticket to Ride", "Yesterday", and "Help!." Although this was their final live appearance on the show, the group would for several years provide filmed promotional clips of songs to air exclusively on Sullivan's program such as the 1966 and 1967 clips of "Paperback Writer", "Rain", "Penny Lane", and "Strawberry Fields Forever".

Although the appearances by The Beatles, Elvis and The Supremes are considered the most famous rock and roll performances on *Ed Sullivan*, several months before Elvis debuted, Sullivan invited Bill Haley & His Comets to perform their then-current hit "Rock Around the Clock" in early August 1955. This was later recognized by CBS and others (including music historian Jim Dawson in his book on "Rock Around the Clock") as the first performance of a rock and roll song on a national television program.
Wikipedia

The '60s were starting to gain momentum. Ever since John F. Kennedy was killed in Dallas, Texas in November of 1963, I started to realize America was not a show called 'Leave it to Beaver'. Also Annette Funicello and Frankie Avalon were not who I wanted to be when I grew up. I started to think outside the box and I could sense others where doing the same as well. Someone out there in the information world was pulling the strings and many of us in the '60s were starting to see there ware men behind the curtain manipulating the way we, as Americans, should think and act.

Leave It to Beaver is an American television situation comedy about an inquisitive but often naïve boy named Theodore "The Beaver" Cleaver (portrayed by Jerry Mathers) and his adventures at home, in school, and around his suburban neighborhood. The show also starred Barbara Billingsley and Hugh Beaumont as Beaver's parents, June and Ward Cleaver, and Tony Dow as Beaver's brother Wally. The show has attained an iconic status in the United States, with the Cleavers exemplifying the idealized suburban family of the mid-20th century.

One of the first primetime sitcom series written from a child's point-of-view, the show was created by the writers Joe Connelly and Bob Mosher. These veterans of radio and early television found inspiration for the show's characters, plots, and dialogue in the lives, experiences, and conversations of their own children. Like several television dramas and sitcoms of the late 1950's and early 1960's (*Lassie* and *My Three Sons*, for example), *Leave It to Beaver* is a glimpse at middle-class, white American boyhood. In a typical episode Beaver got into some sort of trouble, then faced his parents for reprimand

and correction. However, neither parent was omniscient; indeed, the series often showed the parents debating their approach to child rearing, and some episodes were built around parental gaffes.

Comprising six full 39-week seasons (234 episodes), the show had its debut on CBS on October 4, 1957, and then moved to ABC the following year, completing its run on June 20, 1963. Although television production was transitioning from black-and-white to color in the latter years of the show's run, the series continued to be shot with a single camera on black-and-white 35mm film. The show's production companies included comedian George Gobel's Gomalco Productions (1957–1961) and Kayro Productions (1961–1963) with filming at Revue Studios/Republic Studios and Universal Studios in Los Angeles, California. The show was distributed by MCA Television.

The still popular show was canceled in 1963 because the stars wanted to move on. In that year Jerry Mathers was entering his freshman year in high school and actor Tony Dow was about to graduate from high school.

Contemporary commentators praised *Leave It to Beaver*, with *Variety* comparing Beaver to Mark Twain's Tom Sawyer. Much juvenile merchandise was released during the show's first-run including board games, novels, and comic books. The show has enjoyed a renaissance in popularity since the 1970s through off-network syndication, a reunion telemovie, *Still the Beaver* (1983), and a sequel series *The New Leave It to Beaver* (1985–89). In 1997, a movie version based on the original series was released to moderate acclaim, and, in October 2007, TV Land celebrated the show's 50th anniversary with a marathon. Although the show never broke into the Nielsen ratings top-30 nor won any awards, it placed on *TIME* magazine's unranked 2007 list of "The 100 Best TV Shows of All-TIME."

According to Tony Dow, "if any line got too much of a laugh, they'd take it out. They didn't want a big laugh; they wanted chuckles."
Wikipedia

Beach Blanket Bingo is an American International Pictures beach party film, released in 1965 and was directed by William

Asher. It is the fifth film in the beach party film series. The film starred Frankie Avalon and Annette Funicello and also featured cameos by Paul Lynde, Don Rickles and Buster Keaton.

The other films in this series are *Beach Party* (1963), *Muscle Beach Party* (1964), *Bikini Beach* (1964), *Pajama Party* (1964), *How to Stuff a Wild Bikini* (1965), and *The Ghost in the Invisible Bikini* (1966).
Wikipedia

From 1966 to 1968 I started to live the summers in Goleta, California where the campus of UCSB was located. I worked in the county doing different jobs including landscaping, maintenance at the Hope Ranch Riding Club, lifeguard at a dude ranch near Solvang, north of Goleta, and a waiter in several restaurants including the Somerset House in Montecito.

One summer my roommate, Pat, who lived with me in the fraternity house, decided to stay for the June to August break and work as well. One evening he came into the apartment and told me he had tried smoking marijuana with another fraternity brother named Tracy. Both Pat and I had been living in a fraternity house and socializing only with those future upstanding young men and women who would be the leaders of the country in twenty years. Alcohol was the drug of choice and the use of the Mexican grass was not included in their vocabulary or social habits.

Pat invited Tracy to come over to our apartment the next evening and he brought some of the grass so we could all try it. I really had not heard much about marijuana and only knew jazz musicians and blues band players smoked it thus forcing them to wear dark glasses when they played in nightclubs because the stage lights were too bright.

Now the new rock bands of the '60s were taking hold and marijuana plus alcohol was their combined stimulate needed to spark the creative juices in performing and making music. I was about to see what this dried brown bunch of leaves was all about. According to the news reports, based on their lack of knowledge of the drug, I would slip into the world of heavy narcotics because marijuana was just the first step towards a life of an addict.

"For the best result, inhale and hold the smoke in your lungs. After a few seconds, exhale. After a few hits you should start feeling the effects."

Hits? A new word for my drug crazed vocabulary. The process of inhaling on a 'joint' or marijuana cigarette was called a hit and I joined right in with the zig-zag wrapped weed that was being passed around the room between Pat, Tracy and myself.

Zig-Zag is a brand of rolling papers that originated in France. It is marketed in the USA by National Tobacco, in Europe by Republic Technologies, and in Japan by Tsuge Pipes. The Zig-Zag brand produces primarily hand-rolled tobacco related products such as cigarette rolling papers, cigarette tubes and rolling accessories.

Zig-Zag man
The character portrayed on the front of Zig-Zag products, colloquially known as the "Zig-Zag man", originates from a folk story about a Zouave in the battle of Sevastopol. When the soldier's clay pipe was destroyed by a bullet, he attempted to roll his tobacco using a

piece of paper torn from his bag of gunpowder.

In an advertising campaign in the 1960s, Zig-Zag published leaflets with the Zouave facing the viewer (much like Uncle Sam) and the caption, "Captain Zig-Zag wants YOU!" **Wikipedia**

After a few 'hits' I sat on the bed and waited for the effects to take over. Nothing seemed to happen. No clouding of vision and dulling of the senses like one got from beer and other alcoholic drinks.

As I sat on the bed Tracy kept asking me,

"Do you feel anything yet?"

"No!" I answered, "but the bed sure does feel soft."

"Here, try this."

Tracy brought out a candy bar and passed it around the room. Each bite was like the first time I had ever eaten one of these sugar packed chocolate delights from Hershey and my mouth exploded with all my taste buds firing off at the same time. Everything seemed to be happening in slow motion. All my senses were heightened and the bed continued to feel like a cloud I somehow had landed on. I decided to try a somersault on the mattress. I seemed to be floating. All my feelings for the world around me were operating at a new level of awareness. The bed continued to be a cloud of softness and after four or five somersaults, I realized I was under the influence of the drug and I was 'stoned.'

All you baby boomers out there who did not believe the hype of this weed leading you to 'Reefer Madness' and had your own 'first time' experiences, now is the time to reflect. We all had a first time, and this was mine in the summer of 1966.

Reefer Madness (originally released as *Tell Your Children* and sometimes titled as *The Burning Question*, *Dope Addict*, *Doped Youth* and *Love Madness*) is a well-known 1936 American propaganda exploitation film revolving around the melodramatic events that ensue when high school students are lured by pushers to try "marijuana" — from a hit and run accident, to manslaughter, suicide, attempted rape, and descent into madness. The film was directed by Louis Gasnier and starred a cast composed of mostly unknown bit actors.

Originally financed by a church group under the title *Tell Your Children*, the film was intended to be shown to parents as a morality tale attempting to teach them about the dangers of cannabis use. However, soon after the film was shot, it was purchased by producer Dwain Esper, who re-cut the film for distribution on the exploitation film circuit. The film was then reissued under several titles in addition to *Reefer Madness*, including *Dope Addict*, *Doped Youth*, *Love Madness*, and *The Burning Question*. The film did not gain an audience until it was rediscovered in the 1970s and gained new life as a piece of unintentional comedy among advocates of cannabis policy reform. Today, it is in the public domain in the United States and is considered a cult film. It inspired a musical satire, which premiered off-Broadway in 2001, and a film based on the musical in 2005.

Wikipedia

By the summer of 1966 my roommate Pat and I had moved out of the fraternity house and lived in our own apartment. I took a less involved roll in the fraternity and the parties involving getting drunk and getting laid. I was separating myself from the direction and the way these fraternities prepared young men for society and the values they were instilling in them to meet life on the outside. I smoked marijuana more and drank alcohol less and listened to more music coming from the world beyond the hollowed halls of learning.

Several of my fraternity brothers also started to experiment with the Mexican weed. By their senior year they too started to divest themselves from the fraternity life style. How their lives turned out is a mystery to me because I only have contact with my old roommate, Pat, and one other who joined the Church of Scientology.

Chapter Four
A Police Action Called Vietnam

The non-declared war in Vietnam was the number one reason the country was divided into two distinct camps. Pro-war and anti-war citizens clashed in rallies, parades and in political debates. The military draft was also a catalyst that brought the division of views to an explosive head. Young men ages 18 to 25 on the outside of higher education walls who pumped gas at the local Texaco station or started their careers with blue collar jobs were the first to go into the draft. Without an education deferment young men across the country were snapped up, put onto buses, and sent off to the boot camps across the country. Some tried to get married, get their wives pregnant, and hope for a deferment. Some became Canadians and many have lived up north since the 60s. Still others did join and decided it is what Americans do for their country.

In May of 1964 I was returning to California after landing in New York City on a ship from Rotterdam, Holland. I had spent a year in Salzburg, Austria going to school and living with an Austrian family with the name Mastnak. My year abroad was the foundation for my desire to see the world, which came to fruition in 1970 but that is another book. (Living Beneath the Radar)

While traveling across country on Continental Trailways bus line to California on the Golden Eagle, I witnessed the youth of America saying good-by to their parents and girlfriends. They tossed their duffle bags into the storage bin below the seats of the bus and took their place by a window. They showed no expression as to whether or not they thought what they were doing was something they believed in or they were just following the customs of their Midwest communities and families and going off to war. The expressions on their faces were grim and displayed no joy as to what they were about to do.

Being trained to go to war in 1964 was not the same as the year 2012. These men did not have the 'Playstation' commando games used to prepare them in the art of warfare. In their minds, when you got shot you could not push the re-play button on the remote and start over again. This was the real thing and by now the body count coming back from Vietnam was on the rise.

Many of the young men I saw looked like big healthy farm boys. Like their fathers before them who fought in the Korean conflict and

World War II, they were doing what every young man in their town did when their country called. Questioning whether or not they were doing the right thing was never brought up. America had been right in the first two World Wars and the Korean conflict ended as a draw. With two wins and a tie for a recent war track record, no questions were asked whether this was the right thing to do. Uncle Sam wants you and you need to respond. The man behind the curtain continued to pull the strings and direct the country into battle. To question the 'man' was considered 'un-American.'

The **Vietnam War** was a Cold War-era military conflict that occurred in Vietnam, Laos, and Cambodia from 1 November 1955 to the fall of Saigon on 30 April 1975. This war followed the First Indochina War and was fought between North Vietnam, supported by its communist allies, and the government of South Vietnam, supported by the United States and other anti-communist nations. The Viet Cong (also known as the National Liberation Front, or NLF), a lightly armed South Vietnamese communist-controlled common front, largely fought a guerrilla war against anti-communist forces in the region. The Vietnam People's Army (North Vietnamese Army) engaged in a more conventional war, at times committing large units into battle. U.S. and South Vietnamese forces relied on air superiority and overwhelming firepower to conduct search and destroy operations, involving ground forces, artillery, and airstrikes.

The U.S. government viewed involvement in the war as a way to prevent a communist takeover of South Vietnam as part of their wider strategy of containment. The North Vietnamese government and Viet Cong viewed the conflict as a colonial war, fought initially against France, backed by the U.S., and later against South Vietnam, which it regarded as a U.S. puppet state. American military advisors arrived in what was then French Indochina beginning in 1950. U.S. involvement escalated in the early 1960s, with troop levels tripling in 1961 and tripling again in 1962. U.S. combat units were deployed beginning in 1965. Operations spanned international borders, with Laos and Cambodia heavily bombed. American involvement in the war peaked in 1968, at the time of the Tet Offensive. After this, U.S. ground forces were gradually withdrawn as part of a policy known as Vietnamization. Despite the Paris Peace Accords, signed by all parties in January 1973, fighting continued.

U.S. military involvement ended on 15 August 1973 as a result of the Case–Church Amendment passed by the U.S. Congress. The capture of Saigon by the Vietnam People's Army in April 1975 marked the end of the war, and North and South Vietnam were reunified the following year. The war exacted a huge human cost in terms of fatalities (see Vietnam War casualties). Estimates of the number of Vietnamese soldiers and civilians killed vary from less than one million to more than three million. Some 200,000–300,000 Cambodians, 20,000–200,000 Laotians, and 58,220 U.S. service members also died in the conflict.
Wikipedia

In 1965 the idea of the 'police action' in Vietnam not being a justified conflict had no place in the American way of life. The thought process that a young man may have a choice as to whether or not he wants to participate in the jungle battles thousands of miles away, arrived on college campuses across the country that same year. One day at noon a college professor at UCSB stood outside the library in silent protest of the 'police action.' For those readers who didn't know America never declared the Vietnam conflict a war-well they didn't.

For the next four years the professor arrived onto the walkway in the middle of the campus and just stood either eating a sandwich or just standing in the silence. It was a peaceful non-talking protest with no agenda or signs by the professor. For the first year only a handful of students joined him in protest. They also remained in silence not speaking to anyone for the hour they stood. None of them reacted to the taunts and comments made by the fraternity men and sports jocks who had a college deferment and thought such protests were un American. These men who taunted him did not have to face the possibility of being trained, shipped across the world and shot at in a country that never imposed a threat to the US in any way.

In the four years that followed the numbers of silent protesters grew. Some started to bring signs including the body count as it changed each month. All the protesters remained in the silence. A few fraternity men and jocks even joined in by 1968 because they had started to think outside the box.

"Maybe this conflict was not justified. Why should I have to go to the jungles of Vietnam and risk the chance of coming back in a coffin? "

The battle cry of stopping the flow of communism had lost momentum and the man behind the curtain was struggling to come up with another catch phrase or reason young men should risk their lives and die for something they did not believe to be true.

By the time I left college in 1969 I started to separate myself from the protected walls of higher education and independent thinking. The number of silent protestors participating in the peaceful demonstration had reached several hundred. A new wave of protesters had begun on campuses around the country after the shooting of students at Kent State.

The **Kent State shootings**—also known as the **May 4 massacre** or the **Kent State massacre**—occurred at Kent State University in the U.S. city of Kent, Ohio, and involved the shooting of unarmed college students by members of the Ohio National Guard on Monday, May 4, 1970. The guardsmen fired 67 rounds over a period of 13 seconds, killing four students and wounding nine others, one of whom suffered permanent paralysis.

Some of the students who were shot had been protesting against the American invasion of Cambodia, which President Richard Nixon announced in a television address on April 30. Other students who were shot had been walking nearby or observing the protest from a distance.

There was a significant national response to the shootings: hundreds of universities, colleges, and high schools closed throughout the United States due to a student strike of four million students, and the event further affected the public opinion—at an already socially contentious time—over the role of the United States in the Vietnam War. **Wikipedia**

The Black Student Union and the increased number of black minority students who had the brains to attend the 'white sliced bread' campus of UCSB were changing the atmosphere forever. The few black athletic stars who had spent most of their higher education years on the basketball court or football field where being challenged by the women of the BSU. The men had spent their college years bedding down all the pretty white girls wanting to add to their resume the fact they had slept with a black man while in their twenties.

"What's the matter with your own race Uncle Tom? You too good for girls with a little color like you?"

The black girls were relentless and I could see a few of these black athletics starting to question their own values realizing none of the parents of any of the white girls they slept with would allow their daughters to wed a black man no matter what kind of education he had. "Guess Who's Coming to Dinner?" had no place in their household and when this truth became clear to these black men, a change took place. Some eventually became members of the Black Student Union and participated in the rally when Bobby Seale and a few Black Panthers arrived on campus for a little fireside chat in 1968. UCSB would not allow the gathering to be held on campus so an off school location was found and attended by hundreds of students.

Guess Who's Coming to Dinner is a 1967 American drama film starring Spencer Tracy, Sidney Poitier and Katharine Hepburn, and featuring Hepburn's niece Katharine Houghton. The film contains a (then rare) positive representation of the controversial subject of interracial marriage, which historically had been illegal in most states of the United States, and was still illegal in 17 states, mostly Southern states, up until June 12 of the year of the film's release, when anti-miscegenation laws were struck down by the Supreme Court in *Loving v. Virginia*. The film was produced and directed by Stanley Kramer and written by William Rose. The movie's Oscar-nominated score was composed by Frank DeVol.

The film is notable for being the ninth and final on-screen pairing of Tracy and Hepburn (filming ended just 17 days before Tracy's death). Hepburn never saw the completed film; she said the memories of Tracy were too painful. The film was released in December 1967, six months after his death.
Wikipedia

"Soul on Ice" by Eldridge Cleaver was a best selling novel at the time. The story told about the challenges of being a black man in the '60s and the brutal behavior of the police against the black population. I took a Black History class at UCSB in 1968 and the book was required reading for the class.

In 1996 I met Eldridge Cleaver at a retreat in Monterey, California. He was sitting around the fireside and chatting about the role of women in the early church before men took over and cast women as witches. He might have written a book about the subject. He had a small group of women listening to him and asking him questions. He attended the retreat with his daughter and grandchild. I saw him several times during the retreat and was in awe of meeting this leader of the Black Movement in the '60s. He died two years later in 1998.

Soul On Ice is a memoir and collection of essays by Eldridge Cleaver. Originally written in Folsom State Prison in 1965, and published three years later in 1968, it is Cleaver's best known writing and remains a seminal work in African-American literature.

The treatises were first printed in the nationally-circulated monthly *Ramparts* and became widely read (even praised by Norman Mailer) for their illustration and commentary on "Black America." Throughout his narrative, Cleaver describes not only his transformation from a marijuana dealer and "insurrectionary" rapist into a convinced Malcolm X adherent and Marxist revolutionary, but also his analogous relationship to the politics of America. **Wikipedia**

Leroy Eldridge Cleaver (August 31, 1935 – May 1, 1998) better known as **Eldridge Cleaver**, was a writer and political activist who became an early leader of the Black Panther Party. His book *Soul On Ice* is a collection of essays praised by *The New York Times Book Review* at the time of its publication as "brilliant and revealing."

Cleaver went on to become a prominent member of the Black Panthers, having the titles Minister of Information and Head of the International Section of the Panthers, while in exile in Cuba and Algeria. As editor of the official Panther's newspaper, Cleaver's influence on the direction of the Party was rivaled only by founders Huey P. Newton and Bobby Seale. Cleaver and Newton eventually fell out with each other, resulting in a split that weakened the Party.

A reformed serial rapist and racist, Cleaver wrote in *Soul on Ice*: "If a man like Malcolm X could change and repudiate racism, if I myself and other former Muslims can change, if young whites can change, then there is hope for America."

After spending seven years in exile in Cuba, Algeria, and France, Cleaver returned to the US in 1975, where he became involved in various Christian groups (Unification Church, CARP, and Mormonism), as well as becoming a conservative Republican, appearing at Republican events.
Wikipedia

The Black Student Union

The purpose of the Black Student Union, BSU, is to promote activities of common interest, as well as cultural and educational benefits for the African American student body. In addition, the BSU is the "umbrella" organization of many of the African American student organizations, providing a forum for them to voice their differences, goals, and ideas. Furthermore, BSU encourages cooperation between its member organizations and the African American student body.

During the late 1960's and early 1970's, the Black students were experiencing racism from all corners of the university. The only way that the Black students knew how to change their status was to hold protests and rallies that forced the campus to see how passionate they were about getting their respect.

Wikipedia

Robert George "Bobby" Seale (born October 22, 1936), is an activist. He is known for co-founding the Black Panther Party with Huey Newton.

Seale and Newton, heavily inspired by Malcolm X, a civil rights leader assassinated in 1965, and his teachings, joined together in October 1966 to create the Black Panther Party for Self Defense and adopt the slain activist's slogan "Freedom by any means necessary" as their own. Seale became the chairman of the Black Panther Party and underwent FBI surveillance as part of its COINTELPRO program.
Wikipedia

The peaceful protests of the early 60s were being replaced by violence and demands. A group of Black Student Union men took over the main computer building at UCSB in 1968. All the school files and information was being kept on the huge dinosaurs of the early computer world. Microsoft (1975) and Apple (1976) were still a dream in the minds of their creators. The FBI arrived and started taking pictures of all the students standing in the court yard and signing the petitions circulating stating they backed the demands of the men with sledge hammers threatening to destroy the school records. A rumor started saying the signature petitions were actually started by the FBI so they could have a record of who was participating in this un-

American activity. Most did not care and signed anyway.

By 1968, many of the men who had not joined ROTC and laughed at our early morning drills and parade practice were now shining their brass buckles and boot tips. The draft was coming and college deferments were harder to get. Some joined because they knew graduation was just a few years down the road and being drafted as a college graduate with the rank of private or the bar of a second lieutenant was something they could control by joining the ROTC.

The classes in the army at UCSB swelled and the recruiting officers were ecstatic. Saturday drill platoons more than tripled. The burly football players who did not believe in the non-violent thought process of the professor in front of the library and still watched John Wayne movies about World War II, were now dressed in the brown and green neatly pressed uniforms of the army.

In my junior year of college I started to receive a check from the army because I had signed a commitment paper to become a second lieutenant upon graduation. Now that the army had us neatly packaged and ready to go into the service within two short years they started to really show us the true meaning of being in the army and the true intentions of our service.

On a Saturday morning in September we were scheduled to attend bayonet practice on the parking lot near the ROTC classrooms near the west side of campus. The third year students were issued special uniforms used for training in the field and doing things we could not do in our parade pants and shirts. High lace boots and tuck in pants gave us the freedom to move around and complete the exercises planned for that morning.

The young men who were third year ROTC cadets the year before were now the leaders of the program. They all had spent a few weeks at a special summer camp for training. Depending upon how they performed they received their brigade ranks for the following year. The first thing I noticed about these senior cadets who now led the program was the seriousness in which they approached the exercises and drills. The year before they joked about being in the army and continued to make comments like,

"This drill practice every Saturday really sucks. How does learning to march help you walk through rice patties in Vietnam."

Now that they were back in school after completing the summer training they no longer joked about anything. Something had happened to them during those weeks with the army. From the intensity of how they operated the bayonet practice I was not sure if I wanted to make such a commitment to learning how to be a killer.

Upon arrival at the parking lot the first thing that told me we were no longer in the simple parade practice mode of other weekends had to do with the huge sign written in red hanging on the side of the barrack building. On the white sign was the word 'KILL' and dripping off the word, also in red, were droplets portraying blood.

As we were handed our M1 rifles needed to complete the exercise, many of the senior officers seemed to be pumping themselves into a frenzy. They started screaming at us in a manner, which told me the summer camp for ROTC had done a good job in turning these college men into the types of leaders they would need to be on the battlefields of a country far, far away. They were doing their best to get us into this same level of fanatic behavior. They showed us how to lunge with our M1 rifles pretending there was a blade on the end made for killing a human being. We twisted the rifle pretending we had a blade on the end of the rifle and it was entering a body. We then pulled the rifle back towards us. Most of the innards of our imaginary enemy should have remained on the blade. There was no doubt in my mind we were being trained to become killing machines. This was only the first day of that training.

Over the course of the next semester other exercises were carried out to help us survive as potential army soldiers. Crawling under wire on our stomachs with a rifle was the last drill I remember because on this particular workout something pulled in my lower back. By the end of the day I could hardly walk.

I had damaged the lower area of my back while lifting a barbell as I moved it to another room at the end of the previous school year. After a painful visit to a chiropractor who had helped my father get through some of his back issues, I was able to ease the discomfort in this area of my body and return to normal school life. The army exercise had again inflamed the back and a doctor's visit was needed to actually find out what had happened to me.

X rays and a final report told me I had a birth defect, which had been jarred by the lifting of the barbell months before. Now a bone was pinching a nerve. Along with this news came another statement by the doctor. I would not be able to continue my side career towards becoming a second lieutenant along with Forrest Gump and the Lieutenant Dan's of UCSB and get shipped off to Nam after graduation. I was given a letter by the doctor, which described my condition. This letter gave me a medical exit from ROTC and serving in the armed forces.

My first visit was to the Army captain at the ROTC building who handled such requests. He had actually served in Vietnam and had seen fighting in the field, unlike the colonel who was the head officer and had never been overseas in any military action in his life. This captain seemed to have a sympathetic attitude towards my situation and he made the paperwork easy without challenging anything in the medical record. I believed he was not a fan of the Vietnam conflict. Having seen actual combat, he knew many of the young men from UCSB would not live to be 30. He had made the army a career choice but he still did not support the police action in Vietnam.

My exit from an organization in which I had participated for over two years was a real psychological shift in my being. All my military clothing was returned and I was once again a civilian student without the pressures of Vietnam hanging over my head as it was over all those young men either in the ROTC program or those who faced the draft upon graduation.

It was difficult to attend classes and I started to smoke more Mexican weed, now plentiful in most college campuses in America. I believe I was going through some kind of psychological withdrawal and the weed seemed to ease the stress of the situation.

War protests were increasing and so was the body count coming back from overseas. At the end of the school quarter I made my exit from the military. I dropped down to six units

of classes just to say in the system. By the
following semester I again got on track,
changed my major from economics to
geography and started to study the world and
its' different cultures.

Chapter Five
The Draft
If It Bothers You, Close the
Window

This chapter of my post ROTC year and the
required physical the army said I had to take
is also included in my first book, 'Living
Beneath the Radar.' I thought the adventure
to be interesting enough to be repeated at this
time.

The Induction Center Blues

The process of my going through the army
physical exam and draft induction became an
experience Arlo Guthrie might have written a
song about. It was a chaotic time and unlike
Alice's Restaurant you could not get anything
you wanted. If the government drew your
number you needed to go to an induction

center for a complete exam. If you passed the physical you were to be drafted into the Army and shipped off to Vietnam.

I lived in Santa Barbara at the time. I needed to go to the downtown Los Angeles induction center. I received a letter saying two buses, dispatched by the US Army, would pick me up along with forty young men, ages eighteen to twenty-five years old, from a certain locale at about 7:00 am in Santa Barbara.

Arriving around 6:30 I noticed about twenty-five young men who seemed serious and ready to be drafted and serve their country. They already wore military haircuts and all that remained was the physical. Eight men, like myself, held letters from doctors describing some type of physical handicap prohibiting us from serving in the armed forces. The last group of seven men dressed like they just walked off the streets of Haight Ashbury in San Francisco.

This last group I will call the "Santa Barbara Seven." They wore flowers in their hair, tie-dye shirts and bell-bottom pants. A few carried tambourines and musical instruments with them. They were prepared to make this experience a memorable one. I recognized one of them as a UCSB student from a few years before. Several years had pasted since I last saw him. It appeared the members of the group had tuned in, turned on and dropped out following Timothy Leary's directions on how to fight the establishment.

The wait for the busses took a while. Separate groups among the forty men formed. Each of us seemed to gravitate to one another based on haircuts and types of clothing worn. The Santa Barbara Seven became a group by themselves. They started playing some music as we waited for the busses and soon the familiar smell of that plant from Mexico filled the air. A joint made its way through the waiting crowd with an open invitation for anyone to participate. I have never run for political office and I never will. Unlike Bill Clinton, I did inhale.

The busses pulled up about half an hour later. The first vehicle filled with those young men on a mission to join the army, shave their heads and serve their country. The second bus included the eight of us carrying medical papers or letters from our doctors. The Santa Barbara Seven also joined us on the second bus. They were fairly loaded by now and it was only 7:30 am.

The two-hour drive to the Los Angeles induction center from Santa Barbara seemed to take an eternity. During the trip the Santa Barbara Seven continued the music in the back of the bus. Accompanying the music came the continuous draft of thick Mary Jane smoke. It eventually reached the front of the bus and the bus driver. Second hand smoke can be just as powerful as first hand smoke when it comes to Marijuana and I am sure the driver started feeling the effects. He yelled at the Seven in the rear of the bus.

"Put out those joints or I will pull over and throw you all off the bus."

If the same situation happened today the outcome would be very different. I am sure one of the young men would have held out a piece of paper for the bus driver to see. He then would have said,

"I have a doctors prescription so I am legal."

About a half hour later the bus pulled up to the induction center. As I gazed out the window all I could see was a crowd of protesters, filling the sidewalk. Many carried signs expressing their feelings about the Vietnam War. The messages protested against the government sending off young men to be killed in an unjust foreign police action. It looked like a scene from Forrest Gump except this time I found myself written into the script, and life was not like a box of chocolates.

The military draft in our country affected thousands of young men across our country. I remember back to 1964 when I returned to California from Europe. I took the bus across country because I wanted to see what our country looked like up close and personal. The bus pulled into countless small towns in the mid-west and at every stop young men, eighteen years and older, were saying good-by to their girlfriends and families. They were off to the boot camps in different parts of the country. The U.S. was gearing up for the Vietnam conflict. Thousands of these young men did not return from Vietnam and those who did were not given the welcome they thought they deserved. I never supported the war but I feel the country let the returning forces down by not giving them the support they needed so they could re-adjust to civilian life.

All of a sudden the bus door opened and a huge army drill sergeant, probably six feet four inches tall and 275 pounds of prime army conditioning boarded the bus and began barking out orders for the 15 of us in the second bus.

"I want each one of you to stand up and file out of this bus keeping your eyes straight ahead as you enter the building. You will not turn your head to either side. Pay no attention to these protesters who are trying to stop you from serving your country. Is that understood?"

We all stood up and began filing out of the bus and into the building. I can still remember the young women protesters as they approached us shouting,

"They don't own you. You do not need to do this. You are being used to fight a war killing women and children."

Fortunately the walk from the bus to the induction center took only twenty steps. I did my best to keep my head facing forward therefore not ensuing the wrath of the huge army sergeant who gave us orders not to look in any direction other than straight forward. The year 1967 became a time when many young men made a choice and this decision would change their lives forever.

As I entered the recruiting center the movie I found myself playing in just kept unfolding. A young man, with flaming red hair and size almost as big as the sergeant who gave us those first instructions on the bus, started to argue with a smaller army corporal. The red head was yelling,

"You can't tell me what to do. I am not in the army and you can't make me do anything."

Sometimes size makes people do stupid things. This guy may have possessed the size to order people around but he used it in the wrong place. He became outnumbered quickly and the yelling drew the attention of my favorite sergeant. He came over to confront the unwilling citizen. When the sergeant arrived, the face of the almost as big red head changed. His expression said,

"Shit, I think I just blew it."

The sergeant asked the young man to hand him his induction papers. The young man reluctantly gave them to the sergeant. He just stood there trying to put up a front for all of us still standing in line and watching this confrontation play out in the corner of our eyes. Our heads were still facing forward. The sergeant said to the young man,

"Ok, you are free to go. Your papers will be handed in and stamped as refusing to follow directions. You will be notified in the mail as to what the U.S government will do with you."

I may never again witness a young man, as large as he was, lose six inches of height and one hundred pounds of weight as he shrank down and into the body of a small teenager. He started to beg the sergeant to give him back his papers and allow him to go through the physical examination. He knew he screwed with the wrong man and may have made a bad choice. My line kept moving forward. The last time I observed the humbled red head, he was being escorted out of the building and into the crowd of protesters on the street. His life just took another turn and he now needed to live with it.

I do not remember too much of the physical exam. The testing consisted mostly of young men bending over and spreading their cheeks, coughing and being herded into the next room. At the end of all the physical exams a corporal came up to our group and said,

"If anyone possesses medical or psychological paperwork from a doctor, go up to the third floor and wait until you are called."

I knew my winning ticket was about to be called. I possessed a paper and I continued to pass "Go" and collect $200.

The third floor became another scene in this ongoing movie. As I sat on a bench, waiting my turn to see the doctor, I noticed another young man on a bench all by himself. He wore long, black, oily hair and dressed himself in a black leather jacket, black leather pants and a black shirt, which made his pale white skin stand out like a neon sign. Johnny Cash comes to mind when describing the young man and this guy looked like he just emerged from "The Ring of Fire". He rocked back and forth holding his arms across his body. An aura surrounded him with a message attached to it saying,

"Stay away from me! I took a whole lot of pills this morning and I am not going to go into the army. I want them to think I am crazy."

No one went near him and I never saw him again.

My reflection concerning this incident is as follows. Many young men did many different things to avoid the draft and not go into the army. Each had their reasons for not joining or wanting to be a part of the army. The pressures on young men during the Vietnam conflict were tremendous. There are those who are suited for military life and those who are not. The U.S. government, with the draft policy, took everyone. Those men not suited for military life experienced a miserable time. If they were fortunate enough to have received an education they may have found a position doing military office work. The others were put into the field and given a gun. Many never returned.

I held a letter from a doctor. I did not need to choose any of the other options many young men made who were also not military material.

I looked around the room again and noticed an army corporal making his rounds. He proceeded to grab papers out of the hands of each person who waited to be seen by a doctor. He read the letters, and made some negative comment. He tried to get a rise out of each young man. The actions of the corporal seemed to be his job. He allowed no one to escape the torment. He soon made his way to me, grabbed the papers out of my hands and yelled,

"What's the matter with you?"

He read the papers and looked down at me with a look of disgust. He must have practiced the expression each day in front a mirror before he went to work.

"It says here you have a bad back."

"Yes," I answered.

"Can you fuck?" he shot back.

The eyes of all the other young men in the room turned on me. At the age of twenty-two, sex seemed to be everything a male stands for. My answer would determine my manhood in their eyes.

"Yes," I answered. A sigh of relief seemed to come from the other observers in the room.

"Well, if you can fuck you can fight," he fired back. Slamming the papers on the bench next to me, he moved on to the next victim.

Had I been quick enough or brave enough, (or stupid enough) I would have answered,

"You mean when we are in Vietnam all we are going to do is fuck and fight?"

Silence remained the best answer in many situations and I chose not to respond in this one.

The third floor talk with the doctor lasted about thirty minutes. After many questions he brought out a stamp and classified me as 1Y. 1Y is a free pass to live through the Vietnam conflict and not become target practice for the Viet Cong thousands of miles away.

I made my way to the exit of the induction center and out the front door. I looked to my left as I walked onto the sidewalk. No army soldier stood at the door telling me to only look forward. As I viewed the crowd of protesters I was amazed but not completely surprised by whom I saw. Among the crowd stood the Santa Barbara Seven. They were smoking joints and carrying signs with the rest of the American youth I saw while getting off the bus. The Seven never made it into the induction center. They must have stepped off the bus and turned right. Each one made a decision and never looked back. They were not army material. Like the red headed young man who needed to leave the building without taking the physical, these seven men also were about to have their lives change forever. I often wonder how many of them live in Canada today?

Living Beneath the Radar: A Nine Year Journey Around the World

"**Alice's Restaurant Massacree**" is a musical monologue by singer-songwriter Arlo Guthrie released on his 1967 album *Alice's Restaurant*. The song is one of Guthrie's most prominent works, based on a true incident in his life that began on Thanksgiving Day 1965, and which inspired a 1969 movie of the same name. Apart from the chorus which begins and ends it, the "song" is in fact a spoken monologue, with a repetitive but catchy ragtime guitar backing.

Though the song's official title, as printed on the album, is "Alice's Restaurant Massacree" (pronounced mass-a-cree, not massacre), Guthrie states in the opening line of the song that "This song's called 'Alice's Restaurant'" and that "'Alice's Restaurant'... is just the name of the song;" as such, the shortened title is the one most commonly used for the song today. In an interview for *All Things Considered*, Guthrie said the song points out that any American citizen who was convicted of a crime, no matter how minor (in his case, it was littering), could avoid being conscripted to fight in the Vietnam War. The Alice in the song was restaurant-owner Alice M. Brock, who in 1964 used $2,000 supplied by her mother to purchase a deconsecrated church in Great Barrington, Massachusetts, where Alice and her husband Ray would live. It was here rather than at the restaurant—which came later—where the song's Thanksgiving dinners were actually held.

The song lasts 18 minutes and 34 seconds, occupying the entire A-side of Guthrie's 1967 debut record album, also titled *Alice's Restaurant*. It is notable as a satirical, first-person account of 1960's counterculture, in addition to being a hit song in its own right. The final part of the song is an encouragement for the listeners to sing along, to resist the U.S. draft, and to end war.
Wikipedia

Chapter Six
Psychedelic Drugs
Turn On, Tune In, Drop Out

By 1967 a few names in the area of mind expansion began to make the news. The Beatles were leading the way in music with Sergeant Pepper. Donovan was floating down the isles of his concerts along with his flower children followers and the different rock bands including the Jefferson Airplane, Jimi Hendrix, and the Doors were sweeping the airwaves and supporting the anti-war movement any way they could. Several of those great singers of this era including Jimi, Janis, and Morrison of the Doors never made it past the 70s as fame and substance abuse took their lives.

Donovan (born **Donovan Philips Leitch** (born 10 May 1946) is a Scottish singer-songwriter and guitarist. Emerging from the British folk scene, he developed an eclectic and distinctive style that blended folk, jazz, pop, psychedelia, and world music. He currently lives with his family in County Cork in Ireland.

Donovan came to fame in the United Kingdom in early 1965 with a series of live performances on the pop TV series, *Ready Steady Go!*, and his popularity spread to the US and other countries. After signing with the British label Pye Records in 1965, he recorded a handful of singles and two albums in the folk music vein. After extricating himself from his original management contract, he began a long and successful collaboration with leading independent record producer Mickie Most, scoring a string of hits in the UK, the US, Australia and other countries.

His successful records in the 1960s included the UK hits "Catch the Wind" and "Colours" in 1965, while "Sunshine Superman" topped the US *Billboard* Hot 100 chart the following year, and reached number two in Britain. Donovan was the first artist to be signed to CBS/Epic Records by then-new Administrative Vice President Clive Davis, who later became head of the CBS Record empire.

Donovan was one of the leading British recording artists of his day. He produced a series of hit albums and singles between 1965 and 1970. He became a friend of leading pop musicians including Joan Baez, Brian Jones, Bruce Springsteen, and The Beatles. He influenced both John Lennon and Paul McCartney when he taught them his finger-picking guitar style in 1968. Donovan's commercial fortunes waned after he parted ways with Mickie Most in 1969, and he left the music industry for a time.

He continued to perform and record sporadically in the 1970s and 1980s, but gradually fell from favor. His gentle musical style and hippie image was scorned by critics, especially after the advent of punk rock. Donovan withdrew from performing and recording several times during his career, but he underwent a revival in the 1990s with the emergence of the rave scene in Britain. Late in the decade, he recorded the 1996 album *Sutras* with producer and long-time fan Rick Rubin and in 2004 released a new album, *Beat Café*. On 28 September 2010, Donovan was nominated for induction into the Rock and Roll Hall of Fame 2011.
Wikipedia

James Marshall "Jimi" Hendrix (born **Johnny Allen Hendrix**; November 27, 1942 – September 18, 1970) was an American guitarist and singer-songwriter. He is widely considered to be the greatest guitarist in musical history, and one of the most influential musicians of his era across a range of genres.

After initial success in Europe with his group The Jimi Hendrix Experience, he achieved fame in the United States following his 1967 performance at the Monterey Pop Festival. Later, Hendrix headlined the iconic 1969 Woodstock Festival and the 1970 Isle of Wight Festival. He often favored raw overdriven amplifiers with high gain and treble and helped develop the previously undesirable technique of guitar amplifier feedback.

Hendrix, as well as his friend Eric Clapton, popularized use of the wah-wah pedal in mainstream rock which he often used to deliver an exaggerated sense of pitch in his solos, particularly with high bends, complex guitar playing, and use of legato. As a record producer, Hendrix also broke new ground in using the recording studio as an extension of his musical ideas. He was one of the first to experiment with stereophonic phasing effects for rock recording.

Hendrix was influenced by blues artists such as B.B. King, Muddy Waters, Howlin' Wolf, Albert King and Elmore James, rhythm and blues and soul guitarists Curtis Mayfield and Steve Cropper, and the jazz guitarist Wes Montgomery. Hendrix (who was then known as 'Maurice James') began dressing and wearing a moustache like Little Richard when he performed and recorded in his band from March 1, 1964 through to the spring of 1965. In 1966, Hendrix stated, "I want to do with my guitar what Little Richard does with his voice".

Hendrix won many of the most prestigious rock music awards in his lifetime, and has been posthumously awarded many more, including being inducted into the US Rock and Roll Hall of Fame in 1992 and the UK Music Hall of Fame in 2005. An English Heritage blue plaque was erected in his name on his former residence at Brook Street, London, in September 1997. A star on the Hollywood Walk of Fame (at 6627 Hollywood Blvd.) was dedicated in 1994. In 2006, his debut US album, *Are You Experienced*, was inducted into the United States National Recording Registry, and *Rolling Stone* named Hendrix the top guitarist on its list of the 100 greatest guitarists of all-time in 2003.
Wikipedia

Janis Lyn Joplin (January 19, 1943 – October 4, 1970) was an American singer and songwriter from Port Arthur, Texas. As a youth Joplin was ridiculed by her fellow students due to her unconventional appearance and personal beliefs, she later sang about her experience at school through her song *Ego Rock*.

Early in her life Joplin cultivated a rebellious and unconventional lifestyle, becoming a beatnik poet. She began her singing career as a folk and blues singer in San Francisco, playing clubs and bars with her guitar and auto-harp. A heavy drinker all of her life, her favorite drink was Southern Comfort.

Joplin first rose to prominence in the late 1960's as the lead singer of the psychedelic-acid rock band, Big Brother and the Holding Company, and later as a solo artist with her more soulful and bluesy backing groups, The Kozmic Blues Band and The Full Tilt Boogie Band.

Janis Joplin's hits and other popular songs from throughout her short four year career include *Down On Me, Bye, Bye Baby, Summertime, Piece of My Heart, Ball 'n' Chain, Try Just A Little Bit Harder, Maybe, To Love Somebody, Kozmic Blues, Move Over, Cry Baby, Get It While You Can, My Baby, Trust Me, Mercedes Benz, One Night*

Stand and her only number one hit, *Me and Bobby McGee.*

At the height of her career she was known as "The Queen of Rock and Roll" as well as "The Queen of Psychedelic Soul". She was also a painter, dancer and music arranger.

Rolling Stone magazine ranked Joplin number 46 on its list of the 100 Greatest Artists of All Time in 2004, and number 28 on its 2008 list of 100 Greatest Singers of All Time. **Wikipedia**

James Douglas "Jim" Morrison (December 8, 1943 – July 3, 1971) was an American musician, singer, and poet, best known as the lead singer and lyricist of the rock band The Doors. Following The Doors' explosive rise to fame in 1967, Morrison developed a severe alcohol and drug dependency which culminated in his untimely death in Paris in 1971 at age 27, due to a suspected heroin overdose. However, the events surrounding his death continue to be the subject of controversy, as no autopsy was performed on his body after death, and the exact cause of his death is disputed by many to this day.

Morrison was well-known for often improvising spoken word poetry passages while the band played live. Due to his wild personality and performances, he is regarded by critics and fans as one of the most iconic, charismatic and pioneering front men in rock music history. Morrison was ranked number 47 on *Rolling Stone's* list of the "100 Greatest Singers of All Time", and number 22 on *Classic Rock Magazine's* "50 Greatest Singers In Rock".
Wikipedia

I felt a need to include Jimi, Janis, Morrison and Donovan into this era of psychedelic music because of their vast contributions to the sounds of the day.

Dr. Timothy Leary along with his professor colleague Dr. Richard Alpert from Harvard University began experimenting with a substance known in the '60s as LSD or lysergic acid diethylamide. Information about its' effects and what it did to a person were enhanced by interviews given by these men and different people in the area of music. The Magical Mystery Tour came out in the late '60s. Many who wanted to find out the meaning behind some songs such as 'I am the

Walrus' or 'Lucy in the Sky with Diamonds' by the Beatles thought they needed to 'drop acid' to find out the true message hidden in the words. For the few who do not know this simple fact, the letters in the Lucy song spell LSD.

Lysergic acid diethylamide, abbreviated **LSD** or **LSD-25**, also known as **lysergide** and colloquially as **acid**, is a semisynthetic psychedelic drug of the ergoline family, well known for its psychological effects which can include altered thinking processes, closed and open eye visuals, synaesthesia, an altered sense of time and spiritual experiences, as well as for its key role in 1960's counterculture. It is used mainly as an entheogen, recreational drug, and as an agent in psychedelic therapy. LSD is non-addictive, is not known to cause brain damage, and has extremely low toxicity relative to dose, although in rare cases adverse psychiatric reactions such as anxiety or delusions are possible.

LSD was first synthesized by Albert Hofmann in 1938 from ergotamine, a chemical derived by Arthur Stoll from ergot, a grain fungus that typically grows on rye.

The short form "LSD" comes from its early code name *LSD-25*, which is an abbreviation for the German "Lysergsäure-diethylamid" followed by a sequential number. LSD is sensitive to oxygen, ultraviolet light, and chlorine, especially in solution, though its potency may last for years if it is stored away from light and moisture at low temperature. In pure form it is a colorless, odorless, and mildly bitter solid. LSD is typically delivered orally, usually on a substrate such as absorbent blotter paper, a sugar cube, or gelatin. In its liquid form, it can also be administered by intramuscular or intravenous injection. LSD is very potent, with 20–30 µg (micrograms) being the threshold dose.

Introduced by Sandoz Laboratories, with trade-name **Delysid**, as a drug with various psychiatric uses in 1947, LSD quickly became a therapeutic agent that appeared to show great promise. In the 1950's, officials at the U.S. Central Intelligence Agency (CIA) thought the drug might be applicable to mind control and chemical warfare; the agency's MKULTRA research program propagated the drug among young servicemen and students. The subsequent recreational use of the drug by youth culture in the Western world during

the 1960's led to a political firestorm that resulted in its prohibition. Currently, a number of organizations—including the Beckley Foundation, MAPS, Heffter Research Institute and the Albert Hofmann Foundation—exist to fund, encourage and coordinate research into the medicinal and spiritual uses of LSD and related psychedelics.
Wikipedia

Timothy Francis Leary (October 22, 1920 – May 31, 1996) was an American psychologist and writer, known for his advocacy of psychedelic drugs. During a time when drugs like LSD and psilocybin were legal, Leary conducted experiments at Harvard University under the Harvard Psilocybin Project, resulting in the Concord Prison Experiment and the Marsh Chapel Experiment. Both studies produced useful data, but Leary and his associate Richard Alpert were fired from the university.

Leary believed LSD showed therapeutic potential for use in psychiatry. He popularized catchphrases that promoted his philosophy, such as "turn on, tune in, drop out", "set and setting", and "think for yourself and question authority". He also wrote and spoke frequently about transhumanist concepts involving space migration, intelligence increase and life extension (SMI²LE), and he developed the eight-circuit model of consciousness in his book *Exo-Psychology* (1977).

During the 1960's and 1970's, Leary was arrested regularly and was held captive in 29 different prisons throughout the world. President Richard Nixon once described Leary as "the most dangerous man in America".
Wikipedia

I need to also mention Richard Alpert who went on to become a giant force in the '60s and '70s in the area of mind expansion. After his visit to India he changed his direction from using LSD and other drugs to practicing meditation. He became a teacher to those who wanted a spiritual practice in their lives and he separated from Timothy Leary's approach to seeing the world through the use of LSD and other mind-expanding drugs. Many like myself took this approach to seeking a more spiritual life and let go of the Leary path to enlightenment.

Richard Alpert
Youth and education

Alpert was born to a Jewish family in Newton, Massachusetts. His father, George Alpert, was a lawyer in Boston, president of the New York, New Haven and Hartford Railroad, one of the founders of Brandeis University and the Albert Einstein College of Medicine, as well as a major fundraiser for Jewish causes. While Richard did have a bar mitzvah, he was "disappointed by its essential hollowness". He considered himself an atheist and did not profess any religion during his early life, describing himself as "inured to religion. I didn't have one whiff of God until I took psychedelics."

Alpert attended the Williston Northampton School, graduating in 1948 as a part of the Cum Laude Association. He then went on to receive a Bachelor of Arts degree from Tufts University, a master's degree from Wesleyan University, and a doctorate (in psychology) from Stanford University.

Harvard professorship and the Leary-Alpert research

After returning from a visiting professorship at the University of California, Berkeley, Alpert accepted a permanent position at Harvard, where he worked with the Social Relations Department, the Psychology Department, the Graduate School of Education, and the Health Service, where he was a therapist. Perhaps most notable was the work he did with his close friend and associate Timothy Leary. Leary and Alpert were formally dismissed from the university in 1963. According to Harvard President Nathan M. Pusey, Leary was dismissed for leaving Cambridge and his classes without permission or notice, and Alpert for allegedly giving psilocybin to an undergraduate.

Spiritual search and name change

In 1967 Alpert traveled to India, where he traveled with the American spiritual seeker Bhagavan Das, and ultimately met the man who would become his guru, Neem Karoli Baba, whom Alpert called "Maharaj-ji". It was Maharaj-ji who gave him the name "Ram Dass", which means "servant of God", referring to the incarnation of God as Ram or Lord Rama. Alpert also corresponded with the Indian spiritual teacher Meher Baba and mentioned Baba in several of his books.

Later life

In February 1997, Ram Dass suffered a stroke that left him with expressive aphasia, which he interprets as an act of grace. He no longer travels, but continues to teach through live webcasts and at retreats in Hawaii. When asked if he could sum up his life's message, he replied, "I help people as a way to work on myself, and I work on myself to help people ... to me, that's what the emerging game is all about." Ram Dass was awarded the Peace Abbey Courage of Conscience Award in August 1991.

Ram Dass is a vegetarian. In the 1990s, he became more forthcoming about his bisexuality while avoiding labels and asserting that bisexuality "isn't gay, and it's not not-gay, and it's not anything—it's just awareness." At 78, Ram Dass learned that he had fathered a son as a 24-year-old at Stanford, and that he was now a grandfather.
Wikipedia

My roommate, Pat, led by Tracy who first introduced me to marijuana had already tried LSD the week before. I was approached with the opportunity to join the ranks of those who wanted to see the world differently. The famous chemist named Owsley had the best and purest psychological drug out there in the college campus world and Tracy had 'scored' some for our group trip. Each of the participants would be in different locations and at the time we would 'drop' (take) the Owsley tab and meet back at the apartment where Pat and I lived about a half hour later when the acid took effect. I was assured it would take at least 60 minutes before the drug started to alter my perceptions. My first mistake was to believe that statistic.

Owsley Stanley (born **Augustus Owsley Stanley III**, January 19, 1935 – March 13, 2011) also known as **Bear,** was an essential and transitional personality in the development of the San Francisco Bay counter-culture. Spanning the Beat-era years of Ken Kesey's Merry Pranksters scenes, he was equally pivotal to the explosion of 1960's Psychedelia culture. As a brilliant and eclectic crafts-person he eventually became best known under the name of 'Owsley'- the paradigmatic LSD "cook" (underground chemist); a magician-like figure. Stanley's inventive spirit was even further known; Under the professional name of *Bear* he is internationally celebrated an iconic figure (producer, engineer & artist) to psychedelic rock band the Grateful Dead's international fan 'family'— still honored among subsequent generations of Jam band music fans.

Bear rose to prominence initially as an early road manager for The Grateful Dead, a band he met when Kesey had them come to an Owsley Acid test party. Bear's technical interests stimulated the band's developing interest in electronic, acoustic and mystical properties of sound. By 1972 the band enjoyed a pre-eminent reputation as a touring audiophile experience. As their eminent sound engineer, he frequently recorded live tapes behind his mixing board, and Bear was pivotal in "The Dead" becoming the first performers since Les Paul to custom-develop high-fidelity audio components and sound-systems for performance needs. Soon legendary "Dead tours" had evolved around gigantic "Wall of Sound" stacks of Stanley-designed equipment, a highly innovative feat of audio engineering. His expert innovations made it possible for Dead fans to enjoy the full sonic range of the concert even beyond the confines of commercial venues.

Stanley-Bear's unique combination of technical ability and aesthetic ambitions helped develop unprecedented demand for Dead performances. His eclectic interests encouraged The Dead to experiment further afield, playing in dramatic and remote locales. "Dead Shows" gained a reputation for being globe-spanning social-caravans with ambitious service economies. Bear's energies were central to founding both Marin County's high-end music-instrument makers Alembic Inc and concert-sound manufacturer Meyer Sound. And among the first businesses he developed to help subsidize the band's beginnings, his work with popular chemistry earned him a truly iconic status.

Stanley was the first private individual to manufacture mass quantities of LSD. And he did it with panache, evidently more skillfully and consistently than anyone has since. Stanley became most famous as 'Owsley', the clever and iconic yet rarely photographed wizard of the difficult neuro-chemical magic behind LSD. Between 1965 and 1967, Stanley produced more than 1.25 million doses of LSD. These quantities provided a crucial catalyst for the wide popularity of the drug, and the consequent emergence of an anti-authoritarian, anti-war counter-culture. From the 'Sunset Strip Riots' in Los Angeles to the Summer of Love in San Francisco's Haight-Ashbury (which historian Charles Perry described as "the biggest LSD party in history."), "Owsley" as an ad hoc trademark became associated with inexpensive, generously-portioned LSD of reliable professional quality- and thus for "good trips".

Stanley died in an automobile accident in Australia on March 13, 2011.
Wikipedia

The evening we decided to take the LSD I was working for the university in the library with a team of other students. Our mission, 'if we chose to accept it' was making copies of all the library cards in the card catalogue system. We were getting paid so we accepted the job.

A new wing of the building needed another box of cards for students to look up books without having to walk across the library to use the only other card catalogue system in the building. Looking back at this method of finding books, now that the computer age is here, is like seeing man in the 'hunter and gatherer' stage of his development standing in the fruit, meat and vegetable sections of Vons or Safeway in California. It was archaic to go and gather food yourself while someone could do it for you. You just needed some way to pay for the service in some form of exchange. Arrowheads or beaver pelts had value and might work. A lot has changed in the world of electronics since the '60s.

The copy machine we were using to reprint the cards could hold four at a time. Each of us working on the project was responsible for placing a card onto the top loading machine using marks on the glass for positioning each card. We then lowered the top and pushed the print button. A green scanner light swept past the material on the glass and produced the new cards for the new library wing. Another team member used a cutting board to slice the large sheet into 4 individual cards and puncture holes at the bottom so they could go into the catalogue.

The time we had picked for 'dropping' the LSD was around 6 p.m. Tracy said it took an hour or more for the drug to get into the blood stream and produce any effect on the mind.

My job at the library lasted until 7 p.m. and I still had to drive home from campus. Around 6:05 I took a bathroom break and downed the half tablet I agreed to take at this time. I returned to work with the cards and the green light passing over the items needing to be copied and continued to work for the next fifteen minutes.

Maybe it was because I had not eaten for a while or because I had a high metabolism and processed food and drugs quickly but something started to change for me in my attempt to complete the job for the new library wing. The green light passing across the machine started to appear in several dimensions and jumped off the copy machine towards me. The visual show started slowly but by 6:20 I knew the one hour window Tracy had given me to get home before the drug took effect was closing.

At 6:30 I decided to fake having stomach cramps and hoped this excuse would give me the early exit excuse to leave and get home while I still could. Staying focused on the job became difficult when all the parts of the copy machine started to move in ways not intended by the manufacturer. The young men with me were starting to get suspicious of my behavior and inability to concentrate on the job at hand. Right before I played my final exit card and pretended to be sick in order to leave early, the copy machine broke. Can you believe it? We had to stop work early and I was free to find my way home. My guardian angel was still watching over me.

As I made my exit down the stairs of the library, which were also starting to move in waves never intended by the masons who placed them there, I burst out the back door towards the parking lot and was faced with a sea of automobiles which seemed to be coming alive. Somewhere in this vast ocean of VWs and other popular cars of the '60s was my 1964 Corvair, the only rear engine vehicle made by an American company. Ralph Nader, one of the first whistle blowers of the '60s had deemed this car unsafe and the prices dropped quickly allowing college students to be able to afford one. During the time I owned the car all corner turns were done at a slower than normal speed. According to Nader, the Corvair would flip at fast speeds and that was not a good way to end a college career.

Ralph Nader (born February 27, 1934) is an American political activist, as well as an author, lecturer, and attorney. Areas of particular concern to Nader include consumer protection, humanitarianism, environmentalism, and democratic government.

Nader came to prominence in 1965 with the publication of his book *Unsafe at Any Speed*, a critique of the safety record of American automobile manufacturers in general, and most famously the Chevrolet Corvair. In 1999, an NYU panel of journalists ranked *Unsafe at Any Speed* 38th among the top 100 pieces of journalism of the 20th century.

Nader is a five-time candidate for President of the United States, having run as a write-in candidate in the 1992 New Hampshire Democratic primary, as the Green Party nominee in 1996 and 2000, and as an independent candidate in 2004 and 2008. Some people claim that Nader acted as a spoiler in the 2000 U.S. presidential election, while others, including Nader, dispute this claim.
Wikipedia

Walking into the parking lot my mind was going everywhere but my body seemed to know where the red Chevrolet was located. Getting into the vehicle, starting it and driving home would normally be a ten-minute task. Tonight the drive back to the apartment took on a time frame of its' own. It felt like the drive took an hour. As I carefully pulled out of the parking lot and drove along the streets of the neighborhood bordering the campus I observed houses and apartments moving on their foundations. Cars passed me looking like mechanical animals representing the Transformers of the future. People were staring at me as I sped by probably going 20 miles per hour covering the three miles distance to the apartment in record slow motion.

I pulled up to the apartment and found Pat and Tracy in the room and dealing with their observations of the world on the drug made famous by Leary and Albert. Communication was possible and I found out from Tracy and Pat that they had taken the acid earlier than the set time. Pat even took a second dose because he did not feel any effect and wanted to make sure the LSD was working. The double dose seemed to hit him all at once and he had to adjust to the larger amount as best he could.

After an hour or two of experiencing the intense colors, walls moving and sounds amplified because of the heightened awareness the drug seemed to bring to the experience, Tracy suggested we go for a drive and get something to eat. He said he was able to drive. We slowly made our way down the stone and metal stairs to his car parked in front of the apartment and began a journey around the community of Isla Vista where all the students from the university lived and socialized. The neighborhood had taken on a different look and I had to adjust to what I was seeing.

Communication seemed to be telepathic between us. I would hear someone say something but I could not tell if they actually said it or thought it and I was reading their mind waves. People in the streets near the small store where we lived also seemed to be communicating through their thoughts. I was adjusting to the experience but at the same time wondered how long it would last. Food tastes were heightened, life forms radiated energy from their bodies and the rainbow of every hue seemed to explode off the signs and lights from the buildings and houses near the store.

Food was purchased and after a drive around the neighborhood we headed back to the apartment to eat and experience the effects for a few more hours. By sunrise we were slowly returning to our normal perceptions of the world. We decided to drive to the cliffs overlooking the Pacific Ocean a few blocks away and watch the rays of our nearest star bounce off the waters in the Santa Barbara Channel. The sun continued to rise in the east behind the coastal mountain range surrounding Santa Barbara and entertain us with a final light show of nature doing what it did every day. Sunrises would never be the same for me again and I vowed to take more time to watch nature perform whenever I could.

Back to the apartment, goodbyes to Tracy and sleep. I had entered the world of the Magical Mystery Tour and had experienced the universe at an energy level unknown to me through my normal perceptions of life.

Looking back on this first experience and the handful that followed in the next decade, I now see why the expression, 'Turn on, tune in and drop out,' became so popular. 'Turning on' was used to describe the act of getting high, either through psychological drugs or smoking grass. 'Tuning in' was seeing the world differently and slowing down to engulf your being into the beauty and life surrounding us. 'Dropping out' meant we did not need to continue with the direction our society was telling us to take. We did not have to follow the plan the 'man behind the curtain' had laid out for us to blindly follow. We could do life 'our way.' Even Frank Sinatra knew that fact and he did it his way.

I cannot speak for everyone who experienced the '60s but this is what I learned from my LSD trip and those that followed. I was free to do what I wanted to do and the responsibility for my actions was on my shoulders. All living things are made up of energy, which is sacred. I was starting to see life as precious and pulling away from the justifications of any wars, violent protests and actions leading to the end of life.

"Stranger in a Strange Land" became a popular read during this time. 'Groking' something meant your entire being understood a certain truth at a deep level. "Electric Kool-aid Acid Test", "Be Here Now," and "Siddartha" became other books of choice for those who decided to look at life differently. I am sure "War and Peace" continued to entertain those who wanted no part of the movement that provided a path away from a violent solution. Evolution through consciousness expansion was not for everyone.

Stranger in a Strange Land is a 1961 science fiction novel by American author Robert A. Heinlein. It tells the story of Valentine Michael Smith, a human who comes to Earth in early adulthood after being born on the planet Mars and raised by Martians. The novel explores his interaction with—and eventual transformation of—terrestrial culture. The title seems an allusion to the phrase in Exodus 2:22 (in the Biblical Book of Exodus). According to Heinlein, the novel's working title was *The Heretic*. Several later editions of the book have promoted it as "The most famous Science Fiction Novel ever written".

When Heinlein first wrote *Stranger in a Strange Land*, his editors at Putnam required him to drastically cut its original 220,000-word length down to 160,067 words. In 1962, this version received the Hugo Award for Best Novel. After Heinlein's death in 1988, his wife Virginia arranged to have the original manuscript published in 1991. Critics disagree over whether Heinlein's preferred original manuscript is superior to the heavily-edited version originally published. There is similar contention over the two versions of Heinlein's *Podkayne of Mars*.

While initially a success among science fiction readers, over the following years word-of-mouth caused sales to build, requiring numerous subsequent printings of the first Putnam edition. Eventually *Stranger in a Strange Land* became a cult classic.
Wikipedia

The Electric Kool-Aid Acid Test is a work of literary journalism by Tom Wolfe, published in 1968. Using techniques from the genre of hysterical realism and pioneering new journalism, the "nonfiction novel" tells the story of Ken Kesey and his band of Merry

Pranksters. The book follows the Pranksters across the country driving in a psychedelic painted school bus dubbed "Further" (called "Furthur" in the book due to an initial misspelling on the bus' placard), reaching what they considered to be personal and collective revelations through the use of LSD and other psychedelic drugs. The book also describes the Acid Tests, early performances by The Grateful Dead, and Kesey's exile to Mexico.

In 1968, Eliot Fremont-Smith of *The New York Times* called *The Electric Kool-Aid Acid Test* "not simply the best book on hippies… [but also] the essential book." **Wikipedia**

Be Here Now (or *Remember, Be Here Now*) is a seminal 1971 book on spirituality, yoga and meditation by the Western born yogi and spiritual teacher Ram Dass. The title comes from a statement his guide, Bhagavan Das, made during Ram Dass's journeys in India. The cover features a Mandala incorporating the title, a chair, radial lines, and the word "remember". **Wikipedia**

Siddhartha is a novel by Hermann Hesse that deals with the spiritual journey of an Indian man named Siddhartha during the time of the Buddha.

The book, Hesse's ninth novel (1922), was written in German, in a simple, powerful, and lyrical style. It was published in the U.S. in 1951 and became influential during the 1960s. Hesse dedicated *Siddhartha* to Romain Rolland and Wilhelm Gundert.

The word *Siddhartha* derives from two words in the Sanskrit language, *siddha* (achieved) + *artha* (meaning or wealth). The two words together mean "he who has found meaning (of existence)" or "he who has attained his goals". The Buddha's name, before his renunciation, was Prince Siddhartha Gautama. He was Prince of Kapilvastu, Nepal. In this book, the Buddha is referred to as "Gotama".
Wikipedia

These were a few of the books that I came across during the mid '60s to the early '70s. I started to see life from different perspectives and wanted no part of the idea that killing others made you right. War was not an answer. Conquering other countries for their resources did not make sense. I wanted something different and so I continued to search.

Chapter Seven
The Beatles Go To India

The Beatles visited Rishikesh in India in 1968 to attend an advanced Transcendental Meditation CAFÉ training session at the ashram of Maharishi Mahesh Yogi. Amidst widespread media attention, their stay at the ashram was one of the band's most productive periods. Their adoption of the Maharishi as their guru is credited with changing attitudes in the West about Indian spirituality, and encouraging the study of Transcendental Meditation. The Beatles first met the Maharishi in London in August 1967 and then attended a seminar in Bangor, Wales. Although planned to be a 10-day session, their stay was cut short by the death of their manager, Brian Epstein. Wanting to learn more, they kept in contact with the Maharishi and planned to attend his ashram in October, but their trip was rescheduled due to other commitments.

The Maharishi's compound was across from Rishikesh, located in the holy "Valley of the Saints" in the foothills of the Himalayas, and the home to many ashrams. The Beatles arrived there in February 1968, along with wives, girlfriends, assistants and numerous reporters, joining about 60 other TM students, including musicians Donovan, Mike Love of The Beach Boys, and flautist Paul Horn. While there, Lennon, McCartney and Harrison wrote many songs (Ringo Starr wrote one), of which eighteen were later recorded for *The Beatles* (*White Album*), two for *Abbey Road*, and others for solo works.

Starr left on 1 March, after only a short stay; Paul McCartney left mid-March due to other commitments; while John Lennon and George Harrison left abruptly in April following financial disagreements and rumors of inappropriate behavior by the Maharishi, accusations which were made public. Harrison later apologized for the way the Maharishi had been treated by himself and Lennon, and in 1992, he gave a benefit concert for the Maharishi-associated Natural Law Party. In 2009, McCartney and Starr reunited at a concert held at New York's Radio City Music Hall to benefit the David

Lynch Foundation, which funds the teaching of Transcendental Meditation in schools. **Wikipedia**

I remember the changes in music, especially with the 'Fab Four' because some of the songs included Indian chants and other eastern ideas. George Harrison led the shift in thought and became a member of the Hare Krishna sect, spreading throughout the west with ashrams and places for feeding the needy and helping to get the youth off of drugs.

Hare Krishnas
After coming in contact with the Hare Krishnas in 1969, several of the Beatles took interest in the movement. This interest is reflected in songs later recorded by the band and its members.

- The Hare Krishna mantra can be heard sung by George Harrison in his song "My Sweet Lord" (1971) within the backing vocals, and his song "Living in the Material World" (1973) contains the lyrics, "I hope to get out of this place by the Lord Sri Krishna's grace. My salvation from the material world."

Harrison also chanted the Hare Krishna mantra when he was attacked by a man who broke into his home on December 30, 1999. Harrison survived the knife attack, and continued to praise Krishna for the remainder of his life. Of the four Beatles members, only Harrison was actually a Krishna devotee, and after he posthumously received a star on the Hollywood Walk of Fame in 2009, his son Dhani Harrison uttered out the phrase *Hare Krishna* during the ceremony.

•

• The mantra was released as a single by the *Radha Krsna Temple* (1971) on The Beatles' Apple Records label (see Apple Records discography). The album was produced by George Harrison.

•

• The words "Hare Krishna" are included in the lyrics of several of The Beatles and John Lennon songs, such as "Give Peace a Chance" (1969) and "I Am the Walrus" (1967). "Hare Krishna" can also be heard in the backing vocals of Ringo Starr's "It Don't Come Easy" (1971), which was produced by George

Harrison and co-written by Starr and Harrison (although credited to Starr).

- "I Found Out," from *John Lennon/Plastic Ono Band*, released in 1970, contains a verse on Hare Krishna, dismissing it as "pie in the sky." **Wikipedia**

Transcendental Meditation CAFÉ refers to the Transcendental Meditation technique, a specific form of mantra meditation, and to the Transcendental Meditation movement, a spiritual movement. The TM technique and TM movement were introduced in India in the mid-1950s by Maharishi Mahesh Yogi (1914–2008) and had reached global proportions by the 1960s.

The TM technique came out of and is based on Indian philosophy and the teachings of Krishna, the Buddha, and Shankara, as well as the Yoga Sutras of Patanjali, and is a version of a technique passed down from the Maharishi's teacher, Brahmananda Saraswati. The Maharishi also developed the Science of Creative Intelligence (SCI), a system of theoretical principles to underlie this meditation technique. Additional technologies were added to the Transcendental Meditation program, including "advanced techniques" such as the TM-Sidhi program (Yogic Flying).

TM is one of the most widely practiced, and among the most widely researched meditation techniques. Independent systematic reviews have not found health benefits for TM beyond relaxation or health education. Skeptics have called TM or its associated theories and technologies a pseudoscience.

In the 1950s, the Transcendental Meditation movement was presented as a religious organization. The Transcendental Meditation technique was held to be a religion in a New Jersey court case. By the 1970s, the organization had shifted to a more scientific presentation while maintaining many religious elements. The movement now describes itself on a spiritual, scientific, and non-religious basis. This shift has been described by both those within and outside the movement as an attempt to appeal to the more secular West.

The TM movement has programs and holdings in multiple countries while as many as six million people have been trained in the TM technique, including The Beatles, Russell Brand, and other well-known public figures. **Wikipedia**

Chapter Eight
Our Government and Cuba

In 1960 a new president was elected in America. He was the first Catholic president ever voted in by the United States population. I can still remember the words of the conservative non-Catholic neighbors predicting John F. Kennedy would make our nation follow some guy in Italy called the Pope. The reasoning, based on their unfounded fears,

"Kennedy will have to do what the Pope tells him to do because that is what Catholics have to do. We will be run by the head of the Catholic Church in Italy and English will be replaced by Latin or maybe Italian."

I made the Latin and Italian part of the statement up but the fear of having the Pope giving Kennedy orders was not fiction.

People actually believed such garbage. The statement, 'You can fool some of the people all of the time' could not be more true than it was regarding Kennedy and his being a Catholic in 1960. This was the first time I had heard scare tactics used by a political party to try and swing votes in their direction. Today in elections this tactic seems to be a device used all the time.

John Fitzgerald "Jack" Kennedy (May 29, 1917 – November 22, 1963), often referred to by his initials **JFK**, was the 35th President of the United States, serving from 1961 until his assassination in 1963.

After military service as commander of the Motor Torpedo Boats *PT-109* and *PT-59* during World War II in the South Pacific, Kennedy represented Massachusetts's 11th congressional district in the U.S. House of Representatives from 1947 to 1953 as a Democrat. Thereafter, he served in the U.S. Senate from 1953 until 1960.

Kennedy defeated then Vice President and Republican candidate Richard Nixon in the 1960 U.S. presidential election. He was the youngest elected to the office, at the age of

43, the second-youngest President (after Theodore Roosevelt), and the first president to have been born in the 20th century. Kennedy is the only Catholic president, and is the only president to have won a Pulitzer Prize. Events during his presidency included the Bay of Pigs Invasion, the Cuban Missile Crisis, the building of the Berlin Wall, the Space Race, the African American Civil Rights Movement and early stages of the Vietnam War.

Kennedy was assassinated on November 22, 1963, in Dallas, Texas. Lee Harvey Oswald was charged with the crime, but was shot and killed two days later by Jack Ruby before a trial could take place. The FBI, the Warren Commission, and the House Select Committee on Assassinations (HSCA) concluded that Oswald was the lone assassin, with the HSCA allowing for the possibility of conspiracy based on disputed acoustic evidence. Today, Kennedy continues to rank highly in public opinion ratings of former U.S. presidents.
Wikipedia

Cuba became the downfall of this potentially great leader who never was given the needed years to demonstrate his true potential. Fidel Castro had overthrown the corrupt government of Batista on this island nation only a short boat ride from the Florida Keys.

Fidel Alejandro Castro Ruz (Spanish: [fi'ðel 'kastro]; born August 13, 1926) is a Cuban revolutionary and politician, having held the position of Prime Minister of Cuba from 1959 to 1976, and then President from 1976 to 2008. He also served as the First Secretary of the Communist Party of Cuba from the party's foundation in 1961 until 2011. Politically a Marxist-Leninist, under his administration the Republic of Cuba was converted into a one-party socialist state, with industry and business being nationalized under state ownership and socialist reforms implemented in all areas of society.

Born the illegitimate son of a wealthy farmer, Castro became involved in leftist anti-imperialist politics whilst studying law at the University of Havana. Subsequently involving himself in armed rebellions against right wing governments in the Dominican Republic and Colombia, he went on to conclude that the U.S.-backed Cuban President Fulgencio Batista, who was widely seen as a dictator, had to be overthrown; to this end he led a failed armed attack on the Moncada Barracks in 1953. Imprisoned for a year, he then traveled to Mexico, and with the aid of his brother Raúl Castro and friend Che Guevara, he assembled together a group of Cuban revolutionaries, the July 26 Movement.

Returning with them to Cuba, he took a key role in the Cuban Revolution, leading a successful guerrilla war against Batista's forces, with Batista himself fleeing into exile in 1959.

Castro subsequently became Commander in Chief of the armed forces and shortly thereafter became Prime Minister. His involvement in the overthrow of Batista, as well as a suspected relationship with Soviet Premier Nikita Khrushchev, alarmed the United States, who through the CIA organized the failed Bay of Pigs invasion in 1961 to overthrow his government, before proceeding to orchestrate repeated assassination attempts against him and implement an economic blockade of Cuba. To counter this threat, Castro forged an alliance with the Soviet Union and allowed them to store nuclear weapons on the island, leading to the events of the Cuban Missile Crisis in 1962.

Adopting Marxism-Leninism as his guiding ideology, in 1961 Castro proclaimed the socialist nature of the Cuban revolution, and in 1965 became First Secretary of the newly founded Communist Party, with all other parties being abolished. He then led the transformation of Cuba into a socialist republic, nationalizing industry and introducing free universal healthcare and education, as well as suppressing internal opposition. A keen internationalist, Castro then introduced Cuban medical brigades who worked throughout the developing world, and aided a number of foreign revolutionary socialist groups in the hope of toppling world capitalism.
Wikipedia

America dropped the ball after Castro took over Cuba. They did not aid this rebel leader who was trying to return his country back to the people who lived in poverty under the reign of the US backed Batista. We waited too long and before we could help Castro with an influx of money, Russia stepped in with their idea of government based on Communism.

The McCarthy era was not so many years before the changes in Cuba happened and now a neighbor, windsurfing distance from America, was going to practice this form of government in Cuba. The U.S. has made some blunders but not making Castro an ally and giving him support to rebuild his country was the biggest blunder they made in the early part of the '60s. America has spent billions defending itself from the spread of communism after this screw up.

McCarthyism

Originally coined to criticize the anti-communist pursuits of Republican U.S. Senator Joseph McCarthy of Wisconsin, "McCarthyism" soon took on a broader meaning, describing the excesses of similar efforts. The term is also now used more generally to describe reckless, unsubstantiated accusations, as well as demagogic attacks on the character or patriotism of political adversaries.

During the McCarthy era, thousands of Americans were accused of being

Communists or communist sympathizers and became the subject of aggressive investigations and questioning before government or private-industry panels, committees and agencies. The primary targets of such suspicions were government employees, those in the entertainment industry, educators and union activists. Suspicions were often given credence despite inconclusive or questionable evidence, and the level of threat posed by a person's real or supposed leftist associations or beliefs was often greatly exaggerated.

Many people suffered loss of employment or destruction of their careers; some even suffered imprisonment. Most of these punishments came about through trial verdicts later overturned, laws that would be declared unconstitutional, dismissals for reasons later declared illegal or actionable, or extra-legal procedures that would come into general disrepute.

The most famous examples of McCarthyism include the speeches, investigations, and hearings of Senator McCarthy himself; the Hollywood blacklist, associated with hearings conducted by the House Un-American

Activities Committee (HUAC); and the various anti-communist activities of the Federal Bureau of Investigation (FBI) under Director J. Edgar Hoover. McCarthyism was a widespread social and cultural phenomenon that affected all levels of society and was the source of a great deal of debate and conflict in the United States.

Although anti-Communists then felt these were justified, it became an article of faith among many that the entire thing was unjustified (a "witch hunt"), on either (or both) of the grounds (1) that Communism wasn't a bad thing or (2) that those accused of supporting it had not really done so. With the release of the Venona cables, the feeling of justification increased slightly, but the term "McCarthyism" continues to imply a wholly unjustifiable attack.
Wikipedia

In the following years after Cuba became a communist nation the game of 'chicken' took place between the two world powers of the U.S. and U.S.S.R. A failed attack by anti Castro Cuban forces in Florida known as the Bay of Pigs and the Russians attempting to hide missiles into the country brought the fear of a nuclear war to our doorsteps. This was a real time of crisis because the threat was not thousands of miles away. It was only a short boat ride to Cuba and a launched missile towards Washington D.C. could never be countered in time.

The sales of Pepto Bismo were on the rise and all the aliments related to stress were keeping doctors busy in the states. This was the biggest crisis America has had up to date. Pearl Harbor was a huge crisis as well but Hawaii was thousands of miles away and Cuba only a short missile launch from our shores. 9/11 may have surpassed the magnitude of this crisis but that was not until 2001 and a new century.

The **Cuban Missile Crisis** (known as the **October Crisis** in Cuba or **Caribbean Crisis** (Russian: Карибский кризис) in the USSR) was a confrontation between the Soviet Union and Cuba on one side and the United States on the other in October 1962, during the Cold War. In August 1962, after some unsuccessful operations by the US to overthrow the Cuban regime (Bay of Pigs, Operation Mongoose), the Cuban and Soviet governments secretly began to build bases in Cuba for a number of medium-range and intermediate-range ballistic nuclear missiles (MRBMs and IRBMs) with the ability to strike most of the continental United States. This action followed the 1958 deployment of Thor IRBMs in the UK (Project Emily) and Jupiter IRBMs to Italy and Turkey in 1961 – more than 100 US-built missiles having the capability to strike Moscow with nuclear warheads. On October 14, 1962, a United States Air Force U-2 plane on a photoreconnaissance mission captured photographic proof of Soviet missile bases under construction in Cuba.

The ensuing crisis ranks with the Berlin Blockade, the Suez Crisis and the Yom Kippur War as one of the major confrontations of the Cold War and is generally regarded as the moment in which the Cold War came closest to turning into a nuclear conflict. It also marks the first documented instance of the threat of mutual assured destruction (MAD) being discussed as a determining factor in a major international arms agreement.

The United States considered attacking Cuba via air and sea, and settled on a military "quarantine" of Cuba. The US announced that it would not permit offensive weapons to be delivered to Cuba and demanded that the Soviets dismantle the missile bases already under construction or completed in Cuba and remove all offensive weapons. The Kennedy administration held only a slim hope that the Kremlin would agree to their demands, and expected a military confrontation. On the Soviet side, Premier Nikita Khrushchev wrote in a letter to Kennedy that his quarantine of "navigation in international waters and air space" constituted "an act of aggression propelling humankind into the abyss of a world nuclear-missile war".

The Soviets publicly balked at the US demands, but in secret back-channel communications initiated a proposal to resolve the crisis. The confrontation ended on October 28, 1962, when President John F. Kennedy and United Nations Secretary-General U Thant reached a public and secret agreement with Khrushchev. Publicly, the Soviets would dismantle their offensive weapons in Cuba and return them to the Soviet Union, subject to United Nations verification, in exchange for a US public declaration and agreement never to invade Cuba. Secretly, the US agreed that it would dismantle all US-built Thor and Jupiter IRBMs deployed in Turkey.

Only two weeks after the agreement, the Soviets had removed the missile systems and their support equipment, loading them onto eight Soviet ships from November 5–9. A month later, on December 5 and 6, the Soviet Il-28 bombers were loaded onto three Soviet ships and shipped back to Russia. The quarantine was formally ended at 6:45 pm EDT on November 20, 1962. Eleven months after the agreement, all American weapons were deactivated (by September 1963). An additional outcome of the negotiations was the creation of the Hotline Agreement and the Moscow–Washington hotline, a direct communications link between Moscow and Washington, D.C.
Wikipedia

During this time America was going through a complete melt down. People were stockpiling food. I remember whole sections of the canned goods aisles in our Safeway store in La Jolla being empty. It was probably a similar scenario that takes place in the many stores found in the towns in the path of an incoming hurricane either in Florida or along the southern states in that region. Stockpiling water and canned goods is a necessity because no one knows how long services may be cut during one of these natural disasters.

Schools were teaching the children the drill called 'duck and cover'. Students would go under their desks and kneel down while covering their heads in the hope that they would survive a nuclear blast. There is no surviving a nuclear blast but the exercise seems to pacify the false belief that one could live after an explosion by going under your desk and covering your eyes.

Generals were portrayed in movies making calculated guesses as to how many would die after a nuclear war and that we would come out on top because we would have more survivors than the other guy, whoever that may be. Insanity reigned and some of the biggest nuts were calling the shots that put America and Russia on the edge of world destruction. The arms race had begun. Billions of dollars were spent by both countries. Each country made sure they had more missile warheads than the other nation.

Construction companies were building bomb shelters in people's backyards and special news stories were interviewing families who practiced living underground for a week in their nuclear protected home. I can remember getting caught up in the fear frenzy even though San Diego was thousands of miles away from Cuba and the nuclear threat.

"Mom!" I asked one day. "Why haven't we started to build a shelter in our backyard?"

I was in high school at the time and surviving long enough to get laid in college was important to me. The concept of life after a nuclear attack was insane. Those who had a shelter would have to stay underground for years until the radiation in the atmosphere dissipated. This idea had no bearing on the American thought process. When the families came out of the shelters what would they do after a nuclear war? Those who did not have protection would be dead from radiation poisoning. Safeway in town would not be selling fresh produce in the fruit and vegetable sections of the store. Drinking water would not be available and it would be a short matter of time before all the survivors of the initial blast would starve to death.

The human race might survive in the southern hemisphere where Australia, New Zealand and many countries south of the equator were located. I even knew a few college students who where going to make the move to the land of kangaroos after graduation based on the fact that the nuclear cloud of radiation might not reach them way down yonder in the south.

Cold War

During the Cold War, many countries built fallout shelters for high-ranking government officials and crucial military facilities. Plans were made, however, to use existing buildings with sturdy below-ground-level basements as makeshift fallout shelters. These buildings were usually placarded with the yellow and black trefoil sign.

The initial blast of a nuclear attack might well have rendered these basements either buried under many tons of rubble and thus impossible to leave, or removed their upper framework, thus leaving the basements unprotected. The design of the individual shelter would have determined the ultimate result of such occurrences.

The National Emergency Alarm Repeater (N.E.A.R.) program was developed in 1956 during the Cold War to supplement the existing siren warning systems and radio broadcasts in the event of a nuclear attack. The N.E.A.R. civilian alarm device was engineered and tested but the program was not viable and went defunct about 1966. In the U.S. in September 1961, the federal government started the Community Fallout Shelter Program. (A letter from President Kennedy advising the use of fallout shelters appeared in the September 1961 issue of *Life* magazine.)

In November 1961 in *Fortune* magazine, an article by Gilbert Burck appeared that outlined the plans of Nelson Rockefeller, Edward Teller, Herman Kahn, and Chet Holifield for an enormous network of concrete lined underground fallout shelters throughout the United States sufficient to shelter millions of people to serve as a refuge in case of nuclear war.

American fallout shelters in the early 1960s
were sometimes funded in conjunction with
funding for other federal programs, such as
urban renewal projects of the Federal
Housing Authority, examples being
Barrington Plaza, and other development
projects of Los Angeles County Civil Defense
and Disaster Commissioner, Louis Lesser,
and were designed for large numbers of
citizens.

Idealized American fallout shelter from
around 1957.
Wikipedia

The insanity continued and finally the Russians blinked. The missiles were pulled out and the U.S. had won the showdown. By November of 1963 Kennedy was dead. Not supporting the attack on Cuba was unacceptable to powerful men in America and the attack on the mafia by Robert, John's brother, laid the ground work for theories on the assassination of this president. The fabricated theory by the government regarding who killed Kennedy, how he was killed and why, completed the script and changed many people in the '60s, including myself, to never believe the government again without questioning them.

Many in the '60s were starting to see the curtain move and knew someone was behind it pulling the levers and filling the airways with misinformation and untruths. Bumper stickers saying 'Question Authority' appeared and a whole generation from that era never again would blindly follow our elected leaders just because they said it was the 'truth'.

After the crisis was over bomb shelters were turned into bedrooms for children in their teenage years or for storage. If you cannot stand your adolescent child, putting them underground became a good solution. The movie, 'Blast from the Past' took a comical look at these underground bunkers and the paranoid attitudes of Americans at this time.

Blast From the Past

Calvin Webber (Christopher Walken) is a brilliant and eccentric Caltech nuclear physicist, living during the Cold War. His extreme fear of a nuclear holocaust leads him to build an enormous self-sustaining fallout shelter beneath his suburban home.

One night, while he and his pregnant wife, Helen (Sissy Spacek), are entertaining guests, a family friend comes to inform him that John F. Kennedy and Nikita Khrushchev are getting into a debate. The family turns on their television, and watch in horror. When the Cuban Missile Crisis begins, they ask their guests to leave, and they head down into the shelter. Meanwhile, a pilot is having problems with his plane; he is ordered to eject, believing his jet will crash into the Pacific Ocean. Just as the Webbers descend into the shelter, the plane veers off and crashes into the Webber home, leaving their friends and family to believe the family has died.

The family, having seen the resulting fireball just as they lock themselves in their shelter, believe that the unthinkable has happened and that they are the sole survivors of a nuclear war. The locks on the shelter are set for 35 years and cannot be overridden by anyone inside or outside the shelter — for "their own protection" according to Calvin Webber.

A few days after the locks have been engaged, Mrs. Webber goes into labor and gives birth to a baby boy, whom they name Adam. During the roughly 35 years they are down in the shelter, the world above drastically changes, while the Webbers' life remains frozen in 1962. Adam is taught in several languages, all school subjects, dance, boxing, and many other things. The family passes time watching black and white films and kinescopes of television programs via a projector rigged to a television. Adam is given his father's baseball card collection and shares in various companies.

In the present, the timer on the locks releases, and Calvin decides to check out the surroundings above the shelter (in full protective gear), which has turned into a ghetto. He mistakes this for a post-apocalyptic world and wants his wife and grown son (Brendan Fraser) to stay in hiding, but suffers from chest pain. Adam, who is naïve but well-educated, is sent for supplies and help, thus beginning his adventures.

Much of the humor in the film is derived from his being unaccustomed to the lifestyle of the present (such as using the term negro, and believing "shit" is a French compliment), believing "gay" means happy, and finding awe in simple things of modernity. Early on, he meets Eve Vrustikoff (Alicia Silverstone) at a card store, where she works, and where he went to sell his father's classic baseball cards. She stops the store owner from ripping Adam off and is immediately fired. Adam asks Eve to take him to the Holiday Inn, in exchange for a baseball card, worth $4,000. The next morning, at the Holiday Inn, Eve comes to give back the card to Adam, and after a brief conversation, Eve informs Adam that she has to look for a new job. In exchange for $1,000 a week, Adam asks Eve to work for him, she agrees to help him buy the supplies and his search for a "non-mutant wife from Pasadena". Meanwhile, Adam meets Eve's gay housemate and best friend, Troy (Dave Foley), who offers advice and commentary as Adam and Eve fall in love.

Adam continually impresses both Eve and Troy with his array of talents including an energetic swing dance that garners the attention of Eve's rival, Sophie (Carmen Moré), who starts flirting with the café Adam, spurning Eve when he goes home with her. Adam returns later, having admitted to rejecting Sophie's advances and tells Eve about his past. The sheer notion of the story scares Eve into thinking he is a sociopath or psychotic and delusional and she contacts a medical institution to have him committed, which he escapes.

After Adam is gone, Troy and Eve find that he has "millions upon millions, upon millions of dollars" worth of stocks, and the lifestyle they find he has been living seems straight out of the 1960's. Eventually, Eve finds Adam and the two make up, Adam finally introducing Eve to his sheltered parents.

At the conclusion of the film, Calvin and Helen move into a home at the surface that their son has had constructed with the wealth he has acquired from selling stocks, which acquired great value from splits over the years. Only Calvin is informed that the catastrophe they went into seclusion for was in fact a plane crash, for fear Helen would be incredibly angry at her husband for her years of mistaken confinement.

The film ends with Helen at peace with her newfound freedom from the shelter, Adam and Eve engaged to be married, while Calvin, certain that the "Commies" have faked the collapse of the Soviet Union, starts pacing out measurements for a new fallout shelter.
Wikipedia

Castro continued to rule Cuba and dismantled the casinos and hotels of the rich who used to come to his country to party, drink and gamble. Anything that reminded Castro of the past was removed and tourism came to a screeching halt. No more gambling and income from the tourists visiting this island nation. Russia had a new satellite nation under their wing but they had to pay to keep it functioning.

Certain Native American tribes in the states started to see the financial benefit of casinos years later. Today we now have legal gambling across the country located on tribal lands instead of in one state out west. It is ironic to see Native American tribes taking the monies of the white man in the form of legal gambling. Karma seems to work in many ways.

Cuba had fallen to the communist and this laid the foundation for justifying our entry into Vietnam. We had to stop the flow of this type of thinking or capitalism would not survive. The French were pulling out of this southeast Asian country and we were sending in a police force of troops to make sure the communists did not capture the south of the country.

We had saved South Korea so we needed to do the same in South Vietnam. Instead of letting Korea and Vietnam remain divided and let communism collapse onto itself which is now happening in Korea and Cuba, America decided to go to war at the cost of thousands of lives on both sides of the conflict. Old thinking had won out and so began one of the most controversial military actions in the history of the U.S.

Lyndon B. Johnson took over as president and was sworn in the same afternoon Kennedy was killed in Texas. I was living in Salzburg, Austria at the time with a family and going to school in this beautiful Austrian city. The Armed Forces Radio was covering the November 22, 1963 event and people throughout the U.S. still remember where they were and what they were doing. Pearl Harbor, December 7, 1941 must have been the same kind of moment for my parents generation as the Twin Towers on September 11, 2001 was for the 30 to 40 year old of today. The day Kennedy was killed was the moment when I knew something was not right.

Lyndon Baines Johnson (August 27, 1908 – January 22, 1973), often referred to as **LBJ**, was the 36th President of the United States (1963–1969), a position he assumed after his service as the 37th Vice President of the United States (1961–1963). He is one of only four people who served in all four elected federal offices of the United States:

Representative, Senator, Vice President and President.

Johnson, a Democrat, served as a United States Representative from Texas, from 1937–1949 and as United States Senator from 1949–1961, including six years as United States Senate Majority Leader, two as Senate Minority Leader and two as Senate Majority Whip. After campaigning unsuccessfully for the Democratic nomination in 1960, Johnson was asked by John F. Kennedy to be his running mate for the 1960 presidential election.

Johnson succeeded to the presidency following the assassination of John F. Kennedy, completed Kennedy's term and was elected President in his own right, winning by a large margin in the 1964 Presidential election. Johnson was greatly supported by the Democratic Party and, as President, was responsible for designing the "Great Society" legislation that included laws that upheld civil rights, Public Broadcasting, Medicare, Medicaid, environmental protection, aid to education, and his "War on Poverty." He was renowned for his domineering personality and the "Johnson treatment," his coercion of powerful politicians in order to advance legislation.

Despite the failures of his foreign policy, Johnson is ranked favorably by some historians because of his domestic policies. **Wikipedia**

Johnson finished out the term for Kennedy and was re-elected as a president supporting the conflict in Southeast Asia. Johnson did not seek re-election. In 1968 the riots in Chicago between those who protested the war and the old guard in the city who would not put up with anyone speaking out against the establishment, came to a head. People were arrested and killed in the streets of this city and each side blamed the other for starting the battles. TV coverage was much better then. Reporters risked their lives getting footage of the protests between the two ideologies, while dodging rocks and bullets and risking the possibility of a police club finding their head and their film footage being taken and suppressed.

I remember watching the Democratic Convention with my father while on semester break in San Diego where he lived. Dad sided with the authority on the streets using teargas and weapons and I stood behind the group attempting to impact the convention with the anti-war campaign spreading across America. Father and son remained far apart in the battle of ideologies. The US was at war with itself and the man behind the curtain was losing control of the situation quickly.

The **1968 Democratic National Convention** of the U.S. Democratic Party was held at the International Amphitheatre in Chicago, Illinois, from August 26 to August 29, 1968. Because Democratic President Lyndon Johnson had announced he would not seek a second term, the purpose of the convention was to select a new nominee to run as the Democratic Party's candidate for the office. The keynote speaker was Senator Daniel Inouye (D-Hawaii).

The convention was held during a year of violence, political turbulence, and civil unrest, particularly riots in more than 100 cities following the assassination of Martin Luther King, Jr. on April 4. The convention also followed the assassination of Democratic presidential hopeful Senator Robert F. Kennedy, who had been murdered on June 5.

Both Kennedy and Senator Eugene McCarthy had been running against the eventual Democratic presidential nominee Hubert Humphrey.

Chicago's mayor, Richard J. Daley, intended to showcase his and the city's achievements to national Democrats and the news media. Instead, the proceedings became notorious for the large number of demonstrators and the use of force by the Chicago police during what was supposed to be, in the words of the Yippie activist organizers, "A Festival of Life." Rioting took place between demonstrators and the Chicago Police Department, who were assisted by the Illinois National Guard. The disturbances were well publicized by the mass media, with some journalists and reporters being caught up in the violence. Network newsmen Mike Wallace and Dan Rather were both roughed up by the Chicago police while inside the halls of the Democratic Convention.
Wikipedia

Richard Nixon finally became the republican candidate for president having to wait for Kennedy and Johnson to complete their terms in office. A senator from Oregon, McCarthy became the choice of the anti-war movement but he seemed to be the only man in the country operating within the political system who could see the writing on the wall regarding the police action in Vietnam. The Democratic Party and the rest of the country were still blinded by the fact that if they pulled out of the war they would have to count the police action as a loss. The country had a football mentality. Two world war wins, a draw in Korea and a loss in Vietnam would be a 2-1-1 record. The US had not lost before and it was not going to lose this time. The body count continued to rise.

Richard Milhous Nixon (January 9, 1913 – April 22, 1994) was the 37th President of the United States, serving from 1969 to 1974. The only president to resign the office, Nixon had previously served as a US representative and senator from California and as the 36th Vice President of the United States from 1953 to 1961.

Nixon was born in Yorba Linda, California. After completing his undergraduate work at Whittier College, he graduated from Duke University School of Law in 1937 and returned to California to practice law. He and his wife, Pat Nixon, moved to Washington to work for the federal government in 1942. He subsequently served in the United States Navy during World War II. Nixon was elected to the House of Representatives in 1946 and to the Senate in 1950.

His pursuit of the Hiss Case established his reputation as a leading anti-communist, and elevated him to national prominence. He was the running mate of Dwight D. Eisenhower, the Republican Party presidential nominee in the 1952 election. Nixon served for eight years as vice president. He waged an unsuccessful presidential campaign in 1960, narrowly losing to John F. Kennedy, and lost a race for Governor of California in 1962. In 1968 he ran again for the presidency and was elected.

Although Nixon initially escalated the war in Vietnam, he subsequently ended US involvement in 1973. Nixon's visit to the People's Republic of China in 1972 opened diplomatic relations between the two nations, and he initiated détente and the Anti-Ballistic Missile Treaty with the Soviet Union the same year. Domestically, his administration generally embraced policies that transferred power from Washington to the states. Among other things, he initiated wars on cancer and drugs, imposed wage and price controls, enforced desegregation of Southern schools and established the Environmental Protection Agency. Though he presided over Apollo 11, he scaled back manned space exploration. He was reelected by a landslide in 1972.

His second term saw an Arab oil embargo and a continuing series of revelations about the Watergate scandal. The scandal escalated, costing Nixon much of his political support, and on August 9, 1974, he resigned in the face of almost certain impeachment and removal from office. After his resignation, he was controversially issued a pardon by his successor, Gerald Ford. In retirement, Nixon's work authoring several books and undertaking many foreign trips helped to rehabilitate his image as an elder statesman. He suffered a debilitating stroke on April 18, 1994, and died four days later at the age of 81. Nixon remains a source of considerable interest among historians and the public.
Wikipedia

With Nixon as president the Vietnam conflict would continue. Those manufacturers in the private sector selling things to the military continued to get rich by overcharging the government for items purchased. This was their own private retirement system as they stashed away big bucks for a lifetime of golf, multi house purchases and travel. Toilet seats and hammers were sold in the $75 dollar range and these are just the small ticket items discovered in the mishandling of cash spent on the war effort.

The large items, in the form of weapons and aircraft, were being purchased from companies making huge profits in the war game. Generals getting kickbacks were banking the riches being made during the war. West Point graduates continued to advise leaders in our country that war was always the best solution. Do we now see the reasoning for making the military the only option in the name of 'National Defense?'

The body count continued to rise, the anti-war movement continued to grow and the man behind the curtain was laughing all the way to the bank.

Chapter Nine
Civil Rights

On the west coast where anti-war music in San Francisco began and new thought was starting in higher learning centers like Berkley, the south was also going through changes and challenging the status quo. A preacher named Dr. Martin Luther King raised the banner against the unjust treatment of blacks in the south.   The white citizens in the southern states passed Jim Crowe laws. These laws allowed the whites to maintain control of any 'uppity niggers' who thought they should have equal rights in America.

Pressure on the Johnson administration to pass the Civil Rights Act of 1964 brought the explosion to a head. Rosa Parks refused to give up her seat to a white man on a bus and became a symbol of the NAACP and marches by Dr. King in the south. Blacks walked to work and basically shut down the bus systems in Montgomery, Alabama and forced Jim Crowe to take a back seat.

Jim Crowe Laws

The **Jim Crowe laws** were state and local laws in the United States enacted between 1876 and 1965. They mandated *de jure* racial segregation in all public facilities in Southern states of the former Confederacy, with, starting in 1890, a "separate but equal" status for African Americans. The separation in practice led to conditions that tended to be inferior to those provided for white Americans, systematizing a number of economic, educational and social disadvantages. *De jure* segregation mainly applied to the Southern United States.

Northern segregation was generally *de facto*, with patterns of segregation in housing enforced by covenants, bank lending practices, and job discrimination, including discriminatory union practices for decades.

Some examples of Jim Crowe laws are the segregation of public schools, public places, and public transportation, and the segregation of restrooms, restaurants, and drinking fountains for whites and blacks. The U.S. military was also segregated.

These Jim Crowe Laws followed the 1800–1866 Black Codes, which had previously restricted the civil rights and civil liberties of African Americans with no pretense of equality. State-sponsored school segregation was declared unconstitutional by the Supreme Court of the United States in 1954 in *Brown v. Board of Education.* Generally, the remaining Jim Crow laws were overruled by the Civil Rights Act of 1964 and the Voting Rights Act of 1965.
Wikipedia

Rosa Parks: A tired black woman meets a man with a Dream

In life there are events that change the course of direction of nations and societies. A tired black woman, Rosa Parks, refused to give up her seat in the back of the bus to a white man. She was arrested. A man with a dream came together to change the way things were in the south. This event was the most significant and had the greatest influence on the Civil Rights Movement of the '60s.

Rosa Louise McCauley Parks (February 4, 1913 – October 24, 2005) was an African-American civil rights activist, whom the U.S.

Congress called "the first lady of civil rights", and "the mother of the freedom movement".

On December 1, 1955, in Montgomery, Alabama, Parks refused to obey bus driver James F. Blake's order that she give up her seat in the colored section to a white passenger, after the white section was filled. Parks was not the first person to resist bus segregation. Others had taken similar steps in the twentieth century, including Irene Morgan in 1946, Sarah Louise Keys in 1955, and Claudette Colvin nine months before Parks. NAACP organizers believed that Parks was the best candidate for seeing through a court challenge after her arrest for civil disobedience.

Parks' act of defiance and the Montgomery Bus Boycott became important symbols of the modern Civil Rights Movement. She became an international icon of resistance to racial segregation. She organized and collaborated with civil rights leaders, including Edgar Nixon, president of the local chapter of the NAACP; and Dr. Martin Luther King, Jr., a new minister in town who gained national prominence in the civil rights movement.

At the time Parks was secretary of the Montgomery chapter of the NAACP. She had recently attended the Highlander Folk School, a Tennessee center for training activists for workers' rights and racial equality. She acted as a private citizen "tired of giving in". Although widely honored in later years, she also suffered for her act; she was fired from her job as a seamstress in a local department store.

Eventually, she moved to Detroit, Michigan, where she briefly found similar work. From 1965 to 1988 she served as secretary and receptionist to John Conyers, an African-American U.S. Representative. After retirement, Parks wrote her autobiography and lived a largely private life in Detroit. In her final years, she suffered from dementia. In 1999, a lawsuit was filed on her behalf against Outkast and LaFace Records due to their unauthorized use of her name in their 1998 song, "Rosa Parks".

Parks received national recognition, including the NAACP's 1979 Spingarn Medal, the Presidential Medal of Freedom, the Congressional Gold Medal, and a posthumous

statue in the United States Capitol's National Statuary Hall. Upon her death in 2005, she was the first woman and second non-U.S. government official to lie in honor at the Capitol Rotunda.
Wikipedia

Racism from 1960 to 1969

The Civil Rights Act changed the political face of the country forever and shifted the party borders since the act went into effect. Before the Civil Rights Act, which basically made the Jim Crowe laws illegal, the south was a region supporting the Democratic Party. Johnson was a Texan but the passing of the act on his watch was the end of his career as a politician from the south. The southern states became Republican overnight. Lincoln was turning over in his grave at the thought of the south siding with his party, which freed the slaves and attempted to bring equality to men of any color. Now his party had become a group of men led by white supremacists wanting nothing to do with the equal right of men in their region.

The south still wanted 'Good Old Boy' politics in their region of the country. The

Republican Party was made up of the richest Americans who also wanted to maintain the status quo. They decided to switch alliances in order to keep their way of doing business intact. People like George Wallace was seen carrying a baseball bat as he and his KKK followers attempted to stop the integration of college campuses in the south. This act made headlines throughout the country. News coverage was instantaneous and citizens in America could choose sides while eating their Swanson's TV dinners and watching CBS, NBC or ABC news.

Television was bringing the battles on the streets of America into the homes of citizens in the evening news. Pepto Bismol was again seeing an increase in sales as this turmoil was ripping the country apart as well as the stomach lining of people suffering from indigestion. Eating and watching the news was a popular thing to do in the '60s. My only comment about watching the news and eating at the same time is this; 'It may be hazardous to your health.'

Ku Klux Klan, abbreviated **KKK** and informally known as **the Klan**, is the name of three distinct past and present far-right organizations in the United States, which have advocated extremist reactionary currents such as white supremacy, white nationalism, and anti-immigration, historically expressed through terrorism. Since the mid-20th century, the KKK has also been anti-communist. The current manifestation is splintered into several chapters with no connections between each other; It is classified as a hate group by the Anti-Defamation League and the Southern Poverty Law Center. It is estimated to have between 3,000 and 5,000 members as of 2012.

The first Klan flourished in the Southern United States in the late 1860's, then died out by the early 1870's. Members adopted white costumes: robes, masks, and conical hats, designed to be outlandish and terrifying, and to hide their identities.

The second KKK flourished nationwide in the early and mid 1920's, and adopted the same costumes and code words as the first Klan, while introducing cross burnings.

The third KKK emerged after World War II and was associated with opposing the Civil Rights Movement and progress among

minorities. The second and third incarnations of the Ku Klux Klan made frequent reference to the USA's "Anglo-Saxon" and "Celtic" blood, harking back to 19th-century nativism and claiming descent from the original 18th-century British colonial revolutionaries. The first and third incarnations of the Klan have well-established records of engaging in terrorism and political violence, though historians debate whether or not the tactic was supported by the second KKK.
Wikipedia

=**George Wallace**
Wallace was elected governor in a landslide victory in November 1962. He took the oath of office on January 14, 1963, standing on the gold star marking the spot where, 102 years earlier, Jefferson Davis was sworn in as President of the Confederate States of America. In his inaugural speech, he used the line for which he is best known:

"In the name of the greatest people that have ever trod this earth, I draw the line in the dust and toss the gauntlet before the feet of tyranny, and I say segregation now, segregation tomorrow, segregation forever.

The line, based on a bible quote, was written by Wallace's new speechwriter, Asa Earl Carter.

To stop desegregation by the enrollment of black students Vivian Malone and James Hood, he stood in front of Foster Auditorium at the University of Alabama on June 11, 1963. This became known as the "Stand in the Schoolhouse Door". After being confronted by federal marshals, Deputy Attorney General Nicholas Katzenbach, and the Alabama National Guard, he stood aside.

Wallace again attempted to stop four black students from enrolling in four separate elementary schools in Huntsville in September 1963. After intervention by a federal court in Birmingham, the four children were allowed to enter on September 9, becoming the first to integrate a primary or secondary school in Alabama.

Wallace disapproved vehemently of the desegregation of the state of Alabama and wanted desperately for his state to remain segregated. In his own words: "The President (John F. Kennedy) wants us to surrender this state to Martin Luther King and his group of

pro-Communists who have instituted these demonstrations."
Wikipedia

Dr. Martin Luther King, Jr and Malcolm X became the two extremes of the civil rights movement. Dr. King believed in the non-violence approach used by Gandhi in India and Malcolm X appealed to the angry black community who rallied behind the Black Muslims in the states.

Martin Luther King, Jr. (January 15, 1929 – April 4, 1968) was an American clergyman, activist, and prominent leader in the African-American Civil Rights Movement. He is best known for being an iconic figure in the advancement of civil rights in the United States and around the world, using nonviolent methods following the teachings of Mahatma Gandhi. King has become a national icon in the history of modern American liberalism.

A Baptist minister, King became a civil rights activist early in his career. He led the 1955 Montgomery Bus Boycott and helped found the Southern Christian Leadership Conference (SCLC) in 1957, serving as its first president. King's efforts led to the 1963 March on Washington, where King delivered his "I Have a Dream" speech. There, he expanded American values to include the vision of a colorblind society, and established his reputation as one of the greatest orators in American history.

In 1964, King became the youngest person to receive the Nobel Peace Prize for his work to end racial segregation and racial discrimination through civil disobedience and other nonviolent means. By the time of his death in 1968, he had refocused his efforts on ending poverty and stopping the Vietnam War.

King was assassinated on April 4, 1968, in Memphis, Tennessee. He was posthumously awarded the Presidential Medal of Freedom in 1977 and Congressional Gold Medal in 2004; Martin Luther King, Jr. Day was established as a U.S. federal holiday in 1986. **Wikipedia**

The Civil Rights movement lost another great American. By 1968 Dr. King was dead. His speech called, "I Have a Dream", is still today one of the most moving expression of words written down on paper and it needs to be mentioned in this book.

Malcolm X also needs to be mentioned at this time because of his beliefs and attempts to change the status quo. He knew about the men running the country and their racists views and attempted to expose them in the only way he knew how.

Malcolm X (May 19, 1925 – February 21, 1965), born **Malcolm Little** and also known as **El-Hajj Malik El-Shabazz** was an African American Muslim minister and human rights activist. To his admirers he was a courageous advocate for the rights of African Americans, a man who indicted white America in the harshest terms for its crimes against black Americans. Detractors accused him of preaching racism, black supremacy, anti-Semitism, and violence. He has been called one of the greatest and most influential African Americans in history.

Malcolm X's father died—killed by white supremacists, it was rumored—when he was young, and at least one of his uncles was lynched. When he was thirteen, his mother was placed in a mental hospital, and he was placed in a series of foster homes. In 1946, at age 20, he went to prison for breaking and entering.

In prison, Malcolm X became a member of the Nation of Islam and after his parole in 1952 he quickly rose to become one of its leaders. For a dozen years Malcolm X was the public face of the controversial group, but disillusionment with Nation of Islam head Elijah Muhammad led him to leave the Nation in March, 1964.

After a period of travel in Africa and the Middle East he returned to the United States, where he founded Muslim Mosque, Inc. and the Organization of Afro-American Unity. In February 1965, less than a year after leaving the Nation of Islam, he was assassinated by three members of the group.

Malcolm X's expressed beliefs changed substantially over time. As a spokesman for the Nation of Islam he taught black supremacy and advocated separation of black and white Americans—in contrast to the civil rights movement's emphasis on integration. After breaking with the Nation of Islam in 1964—saying of his association with it, "I

was a zombie then ... pointed in a certain direction and told to march"—and becoming a Sunni Muslim, he disavowed racism and expressed willingness to work with civil rights leaders, though still emphasizing black self-determination and self defense.
Wikipedia

Chapter Ten
I Have a Dream
By Dr. Martin Luther King

"I Have a Dream" is a 17-minute public speech by Martin Luther King, Jr. delivered on August 28, 1963, in which he called for racial equality and an end to discrimination. The speech, from the steps of the Lincoln Memorial during the March on Washington for Jobs and Freedom, was a defining moment of the American Civil Rights Movement. Delivered to over 200,000 civil rights supporters, the speech was ranked the top American speech of the 20th century by a 1999 poll of scholars of public address.

According to U.S. Representative John Lewis, who also spoke that day as the President of the Student Nonviolent

Coordinating Committee, "Dr. King had the power, the ability, and the capacity to transform those steps on the Lincoln Memorial into a monumental area that will forever be recognized. By speaking the way he did, he educated, he inspired and he informed not just the people there, but people throughout America and unborn generations."

At the end of the speech, King departed from his prepared text for a partly improvised peroration on the theme of "I have a dream", possibly prompted by Mahalia Jackson's cry, "Tell them about the dream, Martin!" He had first delivered a speech incorporating some of the same sections in Detroit in June 1963, when he marched on Woodward Avenue with Walter Reuther and the Reverend C. L. Franklin, and had rehearsed other parts.
Wikipedia

Whenever I see the black and white footage of the speech played every year around his birthday in January, I always get a sense that King knew he was not going to be around much longer. Dr. King seemed to have knowledge his time was short and he would not be able to travel to 'the promised land' with those who marched with him and sat in

219

the jails after being arrested for demanding the same rights as white men in this country. In the movie, "Gandhi" the same idea was mentioned by one of the followers of this holy man in a loincloth. Gandhi seemed to know his time was short and he would not live much longer.

The battle for civil rights continues in the south today with whites attempting to block the black voters with regulations and the need to show identification. In the west Arizona has continued the battle against Hispanics under the mask of pretending to guard our borders. Anyone who is non-white is subject to a search by the local sheriff and must show identification papers proving they belong in the states.

Dr. King's battle for Civil Rights continues. We are a country of many ethnic and cultural backgrounds. Chinese came seeking work in the gold fields of California and worked on the railroad in the west during the 1800s. San Francisco still holds one of the largest Chinese populations in America and they are held in high esteem with their family values concerning education and cultural accomplishments in music. The Chinese food is also not too bad and very popular throughout the states.

Japanese, Blacks, Native American, Koreans, Mexicans, Europeans and Jews are a majority of the minority cultures living in America today. Civil Rights extends to each individual of these diverse groups of people and the battle began in the '60s with a man with a dream and a tired woman refusing to give up her seat on a bus. To say that any one race or culture should be the one model in place for the rest to follow is a shortsighted thought process. Freedom of religion and speech is what our country was founded upon and the '60s was bringing the battle for these freedoms to a head.

Chapter Eleven
Women's Liberation
And
They Way We Were

'G L O R I A' was not just a song that hit the charts in 1964 by the Van Morrison band but it was a name associated with the women's movement in the '60s as well. Gloria Steinem with the help of many women across the country had become tired of the image that society wanted them to adhere to. The '50s showed the perfect woman with an apron around her waist, a string of pearls around her neck and cooking the perfect meal for her husband when he came home. Her two children could be seen doing their homework in the background around the dinning room table. June Cleaver and her two sons, Wally and Beaver, was the top sitcom show on TV and it became a representation of the life Americans needed to follow for the next generation.

Gloria Marie Steinem (born March 25, 1934) is an American feminist, journalist, and social and political activist who became nationally recognized as a leader of, and media spokeswoman for, the women's liberation movement in the late 1960s and 1970prominent writer and political figure, Steinem has founded many organizations and projects and has been the recipient of many awards and honors. She was a columnist for *New York* magazine and co-founded *Ms.* Magazine. In 1969, she published an article, *"After Black Power, Women's Liberation"* which, along with her early support of abortion rights, catapulted her to national fame as a feminist leader.

In 2005, Steinem worked alongside Jane Fonda and Robin Morgan to co-found the Women's Media Center, an organization that works to amplify the voices of women in the media through advocacy, media and leadership training, and the creation of original content. Steinem currently serves on the board of the organization. She continues to involve herself in politics and media affairs as a commentator, writer, lecturer, and organizer, campaigning for candidates and reforms and publishing books and articles.
Wikipedia

Enough was enough for the women who wanted something different. Gay women were still hiding under the cover of their professions where they could not be detected. Many gay women, like my aunt Julie, went into the army and became nurses. Other fields of employment such as education had always been open but in the '60s many women wanted the same opportunities available to them as they were to men. They no longer wanted to be Rosie the Riveter only when a war came along. Some liked this physical kind of work and resented being bumped when the men returned from war.

The world of executives was an all men's club and few women could break the stereotypes of this organization. Equal opportunities in the work force along with equal pay for performing the same job became the battleground for the women's liberation movement.

The **Women's Liberation Movement** was a political movement, born in the 1960s from Second-Wave Feminism.

It generated mythology almost before it was born such as bra burning - and it was allegedly a matter of deep concern to those within it at the time that its history would allegedly be rewritten by those who weren't in it. Allegedly one important reality was that it is more sensibly seen as a movement of the 1970s and 1980s, not the 1960s, despite allegedly often being described as a 1960s phenomenon.

The term 'women's liberation' allegedly was coined in the early 1960s, when the word liberation was becoming popular, but (for

example) the first Women's Liberation Conference in Britain took place in 1969, at Ruskin College, and its major publications such as *Spare Rib* and *off our backs* not founded until 1970 and beyond.
Wikipedia

The first time I noticed women activists was when they protested the Beauty Pageants with which most of us had grown up. Along with Hugh Heffner and the Playboy Clubs across the country, women were presented as objects, put into skimpy outfits and paraded around in their push up bras. This was not acceptable to this bunch of ladies.

Since I was in my 20s during this time and my hormones were still raging, I did not get on board with their point of view until years later. The one thing many men did support was the burning of bras by Gloria and her followers. This protest was towards the confinement of the clothing business and the lack of opportunities provided by our culture for women with a brain. A twenty-year old man, like myself, loved seeing beautiful breasts allowed to go free under a summer tank top or silk blouse.

A few ladies at UCSB allowed themselves to enjoy this freedom while being chided by the sorority women whose mission it was to uphold the June Cleaver image for women and conduct themselves in a manner approved by society. Bouncing breasts was not a part of that image.

Clothing styles were also changing and the college students were following the trends brought over from England. The Beatles led the way along with other rock groups. Paisley designs, bell-bottom pants and vests became a part of the styles seen on the streets of San Francisco. The hair length of men starting to creep over their shirt collars in the early '60s. It now reached shoulder length. Mustaches and sideburns kept the barbers busy with trimming tools and the ivy-league look all but disappeared except with those refusing to have anything to do with such changes. These individuals would not emerge again until John Travolta started to strut his stuff in 'Saturday Night Fever' with a shift towards Disco.

I began to go through some changes in my college life. Now my hair covered my ears, cowboy boots replaced Converse tennis shoes and I no longer hung out with my fraternity brothers who still clung to Society's Rules of Engagement as to what directions they would take in life. Many desired to become lawyers with a dentist and psychologist in the mix. Business managers and a few teachers rounded out the brothers in the fraternity regarding the job's market.

I realized there was a separation in my thinking with those who believed in the charter of this southern fraternity establishment. The founders were an organization of southern men after the Civil War who refused to adhere to the idea that all men were equal. In the 60s the fraternity still believed in this concept and would not allow any men of color or race other than white, to join their group. Several chapters in more progressive cities like Los Angeles tried to buck the system and lost their chapter status because they pledged a black man.

In our fraternity chapter an oriental man was well liked and considered as a new member. Several of the old guard protested and said the national organization would take our chapter away. They came from redneck communities in California and they were making sure no one of any race other than white would be admitted to the organization. When the vote came for the Japanese man to be turned away, a young man of Jewish decent named Isaacson made a comment:

"Maybe someone should keep an eye on him after he gets the news so he will not commit Hara-kiri."

The real name for the act of Hara-kiri is Seppuku.

Seppuku ("stomach-cutting") is a form of Japanese ritual suicide by disembowelment. Seppuku was originally reserved only for samurai. Part of the samurai bushido honor code, seppuku was either used voluntarily by samurai to die with honor rather than fall into the hands of their enemies (and likely suffer torture), or as a form of capital punishment for samurai who had committed serious offenses, or performed for other reasons that had brought shame to them. The ceremonial disembowelment, which is usually part of a more elaborate ritual and performed in front of spectators, consists of plunging a short blade, traditionally a tantō, into the abdomen

and moving the blade from left to right in a slicing motion.
Wikipedia

This comment from a man who worshiped in a religion that had suffered discrimination for years in the states as well as overseas, put me over the top. From that moment on I knew I could not participate in the racist policies of this group of men. By the following semester I became inactive in my membership and moved out of the fraternity house. I sought men and women with an open view of the world around them and not one based on color or fear of losing their chapter status. I never looked back on this decision. I knew I was making the changes I would need to live in a world outside the protected walls of college life.

I decided to put this fraternity experience into the section of Women's Liberation because I can only comment on what I knew and what I noticed. Even though there were women of color attending UCSB, none I ever saw were members of a sorority. I do remember one Asian girl in one house but other than that the all woman clubs were white, usually from upper middle class families and on the hunt for the perfect husband. I tend to think from this description that the sororities were also southern-based secret societies that held a charter leaning towards discrimination as well as many of the fraternities of the time.

By the late '60s sororities as well as fraternities had dropped in popularity and both organizations were struggling to pledge members in order to keep their way of thinking alive in colleges. The 60s was producing men and women who no longer needed to participate in groups telling them how to live and act. Thinking for themselves and going against the status quo was turning out young men and women who refused to go along with the rules of society just because someone told them they had to. Following their own values and goals as to how they wanted to live their lives was more important to them. A new type of college graduate was emerging from the halls of learning across the country. The old way of blindly traveling the laid out path society had paved for them was disappearing.

After graduation I visited the home of a college friend who lived in Southern CA. He had earned a degree in business and was working for a large firm in the Los Angeles area. He took me to the UCLA library one night because he knew several of our ex fraternity brothers were there every night studying to become lawyers. I had not seen any of them for two years. I was shocked when I saw them. There were five of them and they looked like they had gone through a copy machine for humans that made them look exactly like one another. The clone device called law school was turning out five more lawyers following the same dress codes, haircut style and language exam. These were not the five individuals I remember when they entered college six years before. I said my hellos and left as soon as I could.

Chapter Twelve
Marches

Everyone who had a cause in the '60s got together with others like themselves and marched. Women's Rights, Civil Rights, Pro War and Anti War marches, Marches for Peace, Veterans against the War, and Black Power. You had a cause and you marched. Mohandas Gandhi had set the tone for non-violent marches when he protested the occupation and injustices of the British in India. He eventually ended the 400 years of English occupation in the East in 1949.

Gandhi's March to the Sea

The *Salt March*, also known as the **Salt Satyagraha** began with the *Dandi March* on March 12, 1930, and was an important part of the Indian independence movement. It was a direct action campaign of tax resistance and nonviolent protest against the British salt monopoly in colonial India, and triggered the wider *Civil Disobedience Movement*. This was the most significant organized challenge to British authority since the Non-cooperation movement of 1920–22, and directly followed the *Purna Swaraj* declaration of independence by the Indian National Congress on January 26, 1930.

Mohandas Karamchand Gandhi (commonly called Mahatma Gandhi) led the Dandi march from his base, Sabarmati Ashram near Ahmedabad, to the sea coast near the village of Dandi.

As he continued on this 23 day, 240 mile (390 km) march to produce salt without paying the tax, growing numbers of Indians joined him along the way. When Gandhi broke the salt laws at 6:30 am on April 6, 1930, it sparked large scale acts of civil disobedience against the British Raj salt laws by millions of Indians. The campaign had a significant effect on changing world and British attitudes toward Indian independence and caused large numbers of Indians to join the fight for the first time.

After making salt at Dandi, Gandhi continued southward along the coast, producing salt and addressing meetings on the way. His group planned to stage a satyagraha at the Dharasana Salt Works, 25 miles south of Dandi. However, Gandhi was arrested on the midnight of May 4–5, 1930, just days before the planned action at Dharasana. The Dandi March and the ensuing Dharasana Satyagraha drew worldwide attention to the Indian independence movement through extensive newspaper and newsreel coverage.

The satyagraha against the salt tax continued for almost a year, ending with Gandhi's release from jail and negotiations with Viceroy Lord Irwin at the Second Round Table Conference. Over 80,000 Indians were jailed as a result of the Salt Satyagraha. However, it failed to result in major concessions from the British.

The Salt Satyagraha campaign was based upon Gandhi's principles of nonviolent protest called *satyagraha*, which he loosely translated as "truth-force." Literally, it is formed from the Sanskrit words *satya*, "truth", and *agraha*, "force."

In early 1930 the Indian National Congress chose satyagraha as their main tactic for winning Indian independence from British rule and appointed Gandhi to organize the campaign. Gandhi chose the 1882 British Salt Act as the first target of satyagraha. The Salt March to Dandi, and the beating by British police of hundreds of nonviolent protesters in Dharasana, which received worldwide news coverage, demonstrated the effective use of civil disobedience as a technique for fighting social and political injustice.

The satyagraha teachings of Gandhi and the March to Dandi had a significant influence on American civil rights activist Martin Luther King, Jr., and his fight for civil rights for blacks and other minority groups in the 1960's.

Wikipedia

Dr. King's march on Selma

The **Selma to Montgomery marches** were three marches in 1965 that marked the political and emotional peak of the American civil rights movement. They grew out of the voting rights movement in Selma, Alabama, launched by local African-Americans who formed the Dallas County Voters League (DCVL). In 1963, the DCVL and organizers from the Student Nonviolent Coordinating Committee (SNCC) began voter-registration work. When white resistance to Black voter registration proved intractable, the DCVL requested the assistance of Martin Luther King, Jr. and the Southern Christian Leadership Conference, who brought many prominent civil rights and civic leaders to support voting rights.

The first march took place on March 7, 1965 — "Bloody Sunday" — when 600 civil rights marchers were attacked by state and local police with billy clubs and tear gas. The second march, the following Tuesday, resulted in 2,500 protesters turning around after crossing the Edmund Pettus Bridge.

The third march started March 16. The marchers averaged 10 miles (16 km) a day along U.S. Route 80, known in Alabama as the "Jefferson Davis Highway". Protected by 2,000 soldiers of the U.S. Army, 1,900 members of the Alabama National Guard under Federal command, and many FBI agents and Federal Marshals, they arrived in Montgomery on March 24, and at the Alabama State Capitol on March 25.

The route is memorialized as the Selma To Montgomery Voting Rights Trail, a U.S. National Historic Trail.
Wikipedia

Dr. King continued with non-violent marches in the south and he as well as his followers were met with police dogs, fire hoses blasting them with high pressured water and beatings. Many civil rights marchers were killed and their bodies buried or mutilated in ways unimaginable. Many of those who committed these crimes got away with their conduct and were not brought to justice until forty years later. This was a violent time and the attitudes of the south and some western states fear the races of color even today.

My roommate in my senior year, George, was active in protesting the war and talked me into going to a march on Sacramento, the capital of California. We drove to UC Davis, near the place where the march was to be held. College students from many different campuses had driven to the Sacramento capital to show their support for ending the war.

The year was 1969 and the nation was polarized with those who supported the war and those who did not. Returning war veterans who were missing limbs and suffered losses from their participation in Vietnam also supported the antiwar movement. Signs were painted and handed out and thousands of us started our walk down the road leading to the state capital.

As the march proceeded past the office buildings lining the street many of the people working in these establishments were standing in their windows to observe the march. All the men had removed their coats and they all wore white shirts and a tie and they all looked just the same. Some had made signs to show their disapproval of the march and any attempt to protest the war, which they knew nothing about. They represented the population who seemed to go along with anything our government did and rejected anyone who disagreed with the status quo.

Someone in the marching crowd started to sing the song, "Little Boxes," a famous antiestablishment song made famous by Pete Seeger during the 60s. The middle class working in the offices conforming to anything they were told to do were mentioned in the song. Many of the marchers knew the words and either sang or whistled the tune.

This was the only real march I participated in because by 1970 I had had enough of the way violence started to creep into the antiwar movement and I was off to Europe. That is another story and it ended up as a nine-year journey around the world.

"Little Boxes" is a song written by Malvina Reynolds in 1962, which became a hit for her friend Pete Seeger in 1963.

The song is a political satire about the development of suburbia and associated conformist middle-class attitudes. It refers to suburban tract housing as "little boxes" of different colors "all made out of ticky-tacky", and which "all look just the same." "Ticky-tacky" is a reference to the shoddy material used in the construction of housing of that time.

Wikipedia

The march ended with speeches in front of the capitol building. A few pro-war thugs on the sidewalks near where we marched tried to intimidate the protesters with catcalls and references to the anti-war movement being full of a bunch of homosexuals. A few veterans who had been to Vietnam and fought in the war were in the march. They took the gay references personally and walked over to the catcallers and challenged their inappropriate reference to them and the other marchers. Some of the war veterans were quite large and the skinny verbal intimidators quickly backed off and disappeared into the crowd for protection. A few of those veterans had no time for a nonviolence march after they had homosexual slurs thrown at them. They would have kicked some butt if the sideline catcallers tried to stand their ground.

Marches took place all over the country and well into the '70s. By the time the war ended I had been gone for five years, traveling and living in India and Europe. I just happened to be in Bangkok, Thailand in 1975 when the last of the troops and civilians who supported the Americans were airlifted by helicopter from the roof of the American Embassy in Saigon. The anti-war movement had finally convinced the American public that the police action in Vietnam, which killed thousands of American men and women, was not worth any more lives. The modern score for wars fought by America was now 2 wins, 1 tie and 1 loss. Not until September 11, 2001 would we again participate in another series of conflicts far away. Even today I do not know if we can put either war against the Taliban in Afghanistan or Iraq in a win, loss or tie column. Only time will tell.

Chapter Thirteen
Protesting Through Music

Bob Dylan, Joan Baez and Phil Ochs along with Peter, Paul and Mary were a few of the big names singing war protest songs and celebrating the change in the status quo occurring during this time. Their songs not only made them famous but they will forever have their names attached to the shift in consciousness America was making. Bob Dylan was a giant in the realm of protest music and he is my favorite singer for his musical contributions. 'The Times They Are A-Changin' stands out as one of his most memorable.

I went to a Bob Dylan concert while living in Australia in 1977. He tried to sing some of his new material based on his becoming a Christian. The audience would have nothing to do with it. They booed him until he started to sing his old protest songs again. I guess once you are labeled a protester you are one forever in the eyes of your followers. I never heard Bob Dylan try singing those other songs again.

Bob Dylan (**Robert Allen Zimmerman** on May 24, 1941) is an American singer-songwriter, musician, poet, film director and painter. He has been a major and profoundly influential figure in popular music and culture for five decades.

Much of his most celebrated work dates from the 1960's when he was an informal chronicler and a seemingly reluctant figurehead of social unrest. A number of his early songs such as "Blowin' in the Wind" and "The Times They Are a-Changin'" became anthems for the US civil rights and anti-war movements. Leaving his initial base in the culture of folk music behind, Dylan proceeded to revolutionize perceptions of the limits of popular music in 1965 with the six-minute single "Like a Rolling Stone".

His lyrics incorporated a variety of political, social, philosophical, and literary influences. They defied existing pop music conventions and appealed hugely to the then burgeoning counterculture. Initially inspired by the songs of Woody Guthrie, Robert Johnson, Hank Williams, and the music and performance styles of Buddy Holly and Little Richard, Dylan has both amplified and personalized musical genres. His recording career, spanning fifty years, has explored numerous distinct traditions in American song—from folk, blues and country to gospel, rock and roll, and rockabilly, to English, Scottish, and Irish folk music, embracing even jazz and swing.

Dylan performs with guitar, keyboards, and harmonica. Backed by a changing line-up of musicians, he has toured steadily since the late 1980's on what has been dubbed the *Never Ending Tour*. His accomplishments as a recording artist and performer have been central to his career, but his greatest contribution is generally considered to be his songwriting.

Since 1994, Dylan has published three books of drawings and paintings, and his work has been exhibited in major art galleries. As a songwriter and musician, Dylan has received numerous awards over the years including Grammy, Golden Globe, and Academy Awards; he has been inducted into the Rock and Roll Hall of Fame, Nashville Songwriters Hall of Fame, and Songwriters Hall of Fame. In 2005, the street on which Dylan grew up in Hibbing, Minnesota, was formally re-named

Bob Dylan Drive. In 2008, a road called the *Bob Dylan Pathway* was opened in the singer's honor in his birthplace of Duluth, Minnesota. The Pulitzer Prize jury in 2008 awarded him a special citation for "his profound impact on popular music and American culture, marked by lyrical compositions of extraordinary poetic power." **Wikipedia**

Joan Baez and Bob Dylan (1963)
Wikipedia

Joan Chandos Baez (born January 9, 1941 as *Joan Chandos Báez*) is an American folk singer, songwriter, musician and a prominent activist in the fields of human rights, peace and environmental justice.

Baez has a distinctive vocal style, with a strong vibrato. Her recordings include many topical songs and material dealing with social issues.

Baez began her career performing in coffeehouses in Boston and Cambridge, and rose to fame as an unbilled performer at the 1959 Newport Folk Festival. She began her recording career in 1960, and achieved immediate success. Her first three albums, *Joan Baez*, *Joan Baez, Vol. 2*, and *Joan Baez in Concert* all achieved gold record status, and stayed on the charts for two years.

Baez has had a popular hit song with "Diamonds & Rust" and hit covers of Phil Ochs's "There but for Fortune" and The Band's "The Night They Drove Old Dixie Down". Other songs associated with Baez include "Farewell, Angelina", "Love Is Just a Four-Letter Word", "Joe Hill", "Sweet Sir Galahad" and "We Shall Overcome". She performed three of the songs at the 1969 Woodstock Festival, helped to bring the songs of Bob Dylan to national prominence, and has displayed a lifelong commitment to political and social activism in the fields of nonviolence, civil rights, human rights and the environment.

Baez has performed publicly for over 53 years, releasing over 30 albums. Fluent in Spanish as well as in English, she has also recorded songs in at least six other languages. She is regarded as a folk singer, although her music has diversified since the 1960s, encompassing everything from folk rock and pop to country and gospel music. Although a songwriter herself, Baez is generally regarded as an interpreter of other people's work, having recorded songs by The Allman Brothers Band, The Beatles, Jackson Browne, Bob Dylan, Violeta Parra, Woody Guthrie, The Rolling Stones, Pete Seeger, Paul Simon, Stevie Wonder, Leonard Cohen, and many others. In recent years, she has found success interpreting songs of modern songwriters such as Ryan Adams, Steve Earle and Natalie Merchant.
Wikipedia

Philip David Ochs (December 19, 1940 – April 9, 1976) was an American protest singer (or, as he preferred, a topical singer) and songwriter who was known for his sharp wit, sardonic humor, earnest humanism, political activism, insightful and alliterative lyrics, and distinctive voice. He wrote hundreds of songs in the 1960s and released eight albums in his lifetime.

Ochs performed at many political events, including anti-Vietnam War and civil rights rallies, student events, and organized labor events over the course of his career, in addition to many concert appearances at such venues as New York City's Town Hall and Carnegie Hall. Politically, Ochs described himself as a "left social democrat" who became an "early revolutionary" after the protests at the 1968 Democratic National Convention in Chicago led to a police riot, which had a profound effect on his state of mind.

After years of prolific writing in the 1960's, Ochs's mental stability declined in the 1970's. He eventually succumbed to a number of problems including bipolar disorder and alcoholism, and took his own life in 1976.

Some of Ochs's major influences were Woody Guthrie, Pete Seeger, Buddy Holly, Elvis Presley, Bob Gibson, Faron Young, Merle Haggard, John Wayne, and John F.

Kennedy. His best-known songs include "I Ain't Marching Anymore", "Changes", "Crucifixion", "Draft Dodger Rag", "Love Me, I'm a Liberal", "Outside of a Small Circle of Friends", "Power and the Glory", "There but for Fortune", and "The War Is Over". **Wikipedia**

Peter, Paul and Mary
Manager Albert Grossman created Peter, Paul and Mary in 1961, after auditioning several singers in the New York folk scene. After rehearsing them out of town in Boston and Miami, Grossman booked them into The Bitter End, a coffee house and popular folk music venue in New York City's Greenwich Village. They recorded their first album, *Peter, Paul and Mary*, the following year. It included "Lemon Tree", "500 Miles", and the Pete Seeger hit tunes "If I Had a Hammer" (subtitled "(The Hammer Song)") and "Where Have All the Flowers Gone?". The album was listed in the *Billboard Magazine* Top Ten for 10 months, including seven weeks in the #1 position. It remained a main catalog-seller for decades to come, eventually selling over two million copies, earning Double Platinum certification from the RIAA in the United States alone.

In 1963 the group also released "Puff the Magic Dragon", with music by Yarrow and words based on a poem that had been written by a fellow student at Cornell, Leonard Lipton. Despite urban myths that insist the song is filled with drug references, it is actually about the lost innocence of childhood. On January 14, 1964 they performed on the Jack Benny television program, with the Bob Dylan song "Blowin' In the Wind".

That year the group performed "If I Had a Hammer" at the 1963 March on Washington, best remembered for Reverend Martin Luther King, Jr.'s "I Have a Dream" speech. One of their biggest hit singles was the Bob Dylan song "Blowin' in the Wind". They also sang other Bob Dylan songs, such as: "The Times They Are a-Changin'"; "Don't Think Twice, It's All Right," and "When the Ship Comes In." Their success with Dylan's "Don't Think Twice, It's All Right" aided Dylan's "The Freewheelin' Bob Dylan" album into the Top 30. (It had been released four months earlier.)

"Leaving On A Jet Plane" became their only #1 hit (as well as their final Top 40 Pop hit) in

December 1969, and was written by the group's friend John Denver. It was the group's only million-selling Gold single. The track first appeared on their million-selling Platinum certified Album 1700 in 1967 (which also contained their #9 hit "I Dig Rock and Roll Music"). "Day Is Done", a #21 hit in June 1969, was the last Hot 100 hit that the trio recorded.

Wikipedia

While attending UCSB I was able to see a Peter, Paul and Mary concert at the Santa Barbara auditorium, probably in 1966. They were fun to listen to, up beat and still they had their message of protest in their music. They were a group for the times.

Many readers I am sure went to many of the protest concerts that filled the '60s and have wonderful experiences. I hope this chapter brings back a few of those memories for you.

Before I finish this chapter on music and protests of the 60s I have to include the anti-war production of Hair. I have seen the play three times since 1969, starting with the original production at the Aquarius Theater in Los Angeles: next a production in West Berlin in 1970 and lastly a recent production in Santa Rosa, California in 1998. The musical was one of the best interpretations of the thought process of young Americans in the 60s as they confronted their fears of being drafted and going to war for something they did not believe in. I will let Wikipedia do the rest.

Hair: The American Tribal Love-Rock Musical is a rock musical with a book and lyrics by James Rado and Gerome Ragni and music by Galt MacDermot. A product of the hippie counter-culture and sexual revolution of the 1960s, several of its songs became anthems of the anti-Vietnam War peace movement. The musical's profanity, its depiction of the use of illegal drugs, its treatment of sexuality, its irreverence for the American flag, and its nude scene caused much comment and controversy. The musical broke new ground in musical theatre by defining the genre of "rock musical", using a racially integrated cast, and inviting the audience onstage for a "Be-In" finale.

Hair tells the story of the "tribe", a group of politically active, long-haired hippies of the "Age of Aquarius" living a bohemian life in New York City and fighting against conscription into the Vietnam War. Claude, his good friend Berger, their roommate Sheila and their friends struggle to balance their young lives, loves and the sexual revolution with their rebellion against the war and their conservative parents and society. Ultimately, Claude must decide whether to resist the draft as his friends have done, or to succumb to the pressures of his parents (and conservative

America) to serve in Vietnam, compromising his pacifistic principles and risking his life.

After an Off-Broadway debut in October 1967 at Joseph Papp's Public Theater and a subsequent run in a midtown discothèque space, the show opened on Broadway in April 1968 and ran for 1,750 performances. Simultaneous productions in cities across the United States and Europe followed shortly thereafter, including a successful London production that ran for 1,997 performances. Since then, numerous productions have been staged around the world, spawning dozens of recordings of the musical, including the 3 million-selling original Broadway cast recording.

Some of the songs from its score became Top 10 hits, and a feature film adaptation was released in 1979. A Broadway revival opened on March 31, 2009, earning strong reviews and winning the Tony Award and Drama Desk Award for best revival of a musical. In 2008, *Time* magazine wrote, "Today *Hair* seems, if anything, more daring than ever."

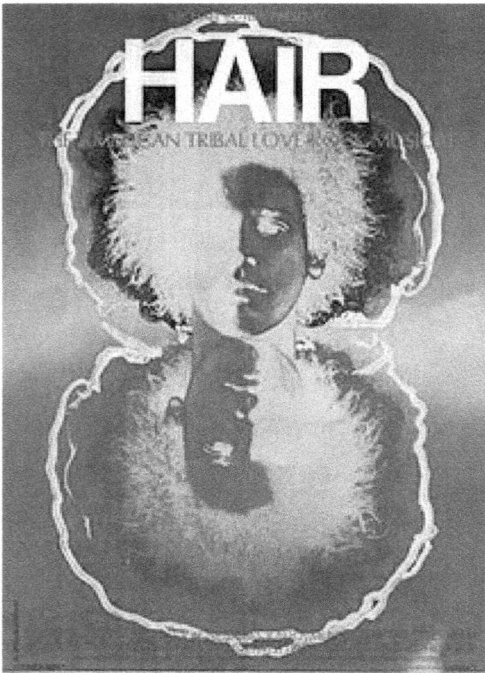

BILTMORE THEATER
261 WEST 47TH STREET, 582-5340

Wikipedia

Chapter Fourteen
Sports in the '60s

During the '60s there were many different
athletes who stood up against the status quo
of this country and could no longer allow
things to continue and turn their heads away
from the injustices happening in society.
Cassius Clay became the world champion
boxer by defeating Sunny Liston who was the
254

world champion at the time. Cassius became the youngest boxer at that time to hold the crown.

After becoming the heavyweight-boxing king he declared his conversion to Islam, which shocked the world of sports and Christian America. A Muslim as the boxing champion was too much for those who were afraid of other religions. The army tried to draft Clay who by now had changed his name to Muhammad Ali but the world champion stood up to the government and refused to enter the army based on his religious beliefs.

Muhammad Ali (born **Cassius Marcellus Clay, Jr.**; January 17, 1942) is an American former professional boxer, philanthropist and social activist. Considered a cultural icon, Ali was both idolized and vilified.

Originally known as Cassius Clay, Ali changed his name after joining the Nation of Islam in 1964, subsequently converting to Sunni Islam in 1975, and more recently practicing Sufism. In 1967, three years after Ali had won the World Heavyweight Championship, he was publicly vilified for his refusal to be conscripted into the U.S.

military, based on his religious beliefs and opposition to the Vietnam War. Ali stated, "I ain't got no quarrel with them Viet Cong. No Viet Cong ever called me nigger" – one of the more telling remarks of the era.

Widespread protests against the Vietnam War had not yet begun, but with that one phrase, Ali articulated the reason to oppose the war for a generation of young Americans, and his words served as a touchstone for the racial and antiwar upheavals that would rock the 1960's. Ali's example inspired Martin Luther King Jr. – who had been reluctant to alienate the Johnson Administration and its support of the civil rights agenda – to voice his own opposition to the war for the first time.

Ali would eventually be arrested and found guilty on draft evasion charges; he was stripped of his boxing title, and his boxing license was suspended. He was not imprisoned, but did not fight again for nearly four years while his appeal worked its way up to the U.S. Supreme Court, where it was eventually successful. Ali would go on to become the first and only three-time lineal World Heavyweight Champion.

Nicknamed "The Greatest," Ali was involved in several historic boxing matches. Notable among these were three with rival Joe Frazier, which are considered among the greatest in boxing history, and one with George Foreman, where he finally regained his stripped titles seven years later. Ali was well known for his unorthodox fighting style, which he described as "float like a butterfly, sting like a bee", and employing techniques such as the Ali Shuffle and the rope-a-dope.

Ali had brought beauty and grace to the most uncompromising of sports and through the wonderful excesses of skill and character, he had become the most famous athlete in the world. He was also known for his pre-match hype, where he would "trash talk" opponents, often with rhymes.

In 1999, Ali was crowned "Sportsman of the Century" by *Sports Illustrated* and "Sports Personality of the Century" by the *BBC*. **Wikipedia**

I crossed paths with "The Greatest" in Phoenix, Arizona in 2009 while writing my first book, '**Living Beneath the Radar.**' It was Valentine's Day and Ali was with his wife and a group of people at a jazz nightclub. By now the damage to this man due to the sport of boxing had reduced his ability to communicate. I talked to his wife and told her the story of how he had helped me cross the border from Thailand to Malaysia in 1975. The story went like this.

The Great Crossing

At the border of Thailand and Malaysia a situation arose which is another story worth repeating. The date, June 30, 1975, became an important time in sports. Pavitra (my first wife) and I left the Thailand section of the border and entered the Malaysian border immigration office.

Upon entering the building I noticed many young westerners sitting around as though they were waiting for something to happen. Whatever they were waiting for was taking a long time to happen. I talked to one of the American travelers. He said the border guards made all bearded men and travelers with long hair sit along the wall. No visas were being granted.

Malaysia did not like hippies coming into their country. The guards hoped these western weirdoes would change their minds about traveling in Malaysia. In this part of the world, guards and police have the power over one's ability to move.

I walked over to the immigration desk and noticed about four or five young men in uniform sitting around and talking with each other. They did nothing in the way of moving along the increasing numbers of western travelers sitting along the wall. The young guardians of Malaysia were listening to the radio and it sounded like a sports event.

All of a sudden I remembered from reading a paper in Bangkok, this date, June 30, 1975 was the day Muhammad Ali fought Joe Bugner in Kuala Lumpur, Malaysia. For all you non-sports fans, or people just too young to remember, the fight with Bugner preceded the "Thrilla in Manila" by three months. If you do not know what the "Thrilla in Manila" is then Google it. The excitement regarding the fight happening at the moment pertained to the fact it took place in the country Pavitra and I attempted to enter. I asked one of the border guards,

"Who is winning the fight?"

He looked at me in an inquisitive way. His expression told me he did not understand everything I said. I pointed to the little radio all the guards were listening to and stepped back from the counter. I raised my arms in a boxing position as though I wanted to take them all on and said again,

"Who is winning the fight?"

One of the guards, who spoke the most broken English, answered,

"Why? Who you like?"

He realized my movements and question referred to the boxing match he and the other guards were listening to. My answer in the next moment would determine how fast I crossed into the country of Malaysia.

"Muhammad Ali" I answered.

"You like Muhammad Ali?" she shot back at me.

"Of course I like Muhammad Ali." I answered. "He is the best."

I limited my use of adjectives to describe the best fighter of all time because too many words get lost in translation. The short statement I gave seemed to be the correct answer to the "Sixty Four Thousand Dollar Question." This is another reference to trivia anyone fifty years old or younger might not have knowledge.

The guard said something to the other border guards in their native tongue. All at once they all started to jump up and down like they just won the Malaysian lottery. The connection between the guards and the fight is as follows. Malaysia is a Muslim country and Muhammad Ali converted to Islam years before. Ali became a Muslim while fighting the American government. The U.S. tried to draft Muhammad into the military and send him to Viet Nam, a war Ali stood against and publicly voiced his opposition. After stripping Ali of his title and his ability to fight in the States, several boxing matches were set up in different foreign countries. All the best fighters wanted to take on Ali. The fights took place in foreign Muslim countries and became big news as well as big money makers.

The match today took place in Malaysia and everyone here wanted Muhammad Ali to win. All the guards came over to the counter and started practicing their own broken English on me in an attempt to show their joy in the fact I liked Muhammad Ali. To them Ali remained a sport hero for their country and religion. One of the guards said,

"Give me passport."

He took Pavitra's and my passport, stamped them, handed them back and said,

"You go now."

He pointed to the train waiting to take us to the next town in Malaysia.

As this incident unfolded all the other travelers, waiting along the walls of the building for hours in order to get a stamp in their passport, looked at Pavitra and me as we exited the building. Their mouths hung open in shock. I could not tell if any of them overheard the exchange with the guards or if the name, Muhammad Ali, meant anything to them. This is one time it paid to be a sports fan and root for the "right" winning player.

"Living Beneath the Radar"

After telling Mrs. Ali the story she thanked me and told me about her travels with her husband to the many Islamic countries around the world where they were treated with dignity and respect. He was still the sports hero of those who worshipped as a Muslim and respected for his courage to stand up to the American government who took away his championship belt and stopped him from fighting for four years.

Another great athlete in the 60's who converted to the Muslim religion was Lew Alcindor.

Kareem Abdul-Jabbar (born **Ferdinand Lewis Alcindor, Jr.,** April 16, 1947) is a retired American professional basketball player. He is the NBA's all-time leading scorer, with 38,387 points. During his career with the NBA's

Milwaukee Bucks and Los Angeles Lakers from 1969 to 1989, Abdul-Jabbar won six

NBA championships and a record six regular season MVP Awards. In college at UCLA, he played on three consecutive national championship teams, and his high school team won 71 consecutive games. At the time of his retirement, Abdul-Jabbar was the NBA's all-time leader in points scored, games played, minutes played, field goals made, field goal attempts, blocked shots, defensive rebounds, and personal fouls. Abdul-Jabbar also has been an actor, basketball coach and an author.

Speaking about the thinking behind his change of name when he converted to Islam he said to *Playboy* that he was "latching on to something that was part of my heritage, because many of the slaves who were brought here were Muslims. My family was brought to America by a French planter named Alcindor, who came here from Trinidad in the 18th century. My people were Yoruba, and their culture survived slavery (...)

My father found out about that when I was a kid, and it gave me all I needed to know that, hey, I was somebody, even if nobody else knew about it. When I was a kid, no one would believe anything positive that you could say about black people. And that's a terrible burden on black people, because they don't have an accurate idea of their history, which has been either suppressed or distorted."

Abdul-Jabbar reached a settlement after suing Miami Dolphins running back Karim Abdul-Jabbar (now Abdul-Karim al-Jabbar, born Sharmon Shah) because he felt Karim was sponging off the name he made famous by having the Abdul-Jabbar moniker and number 33 on his Dolphins jersey, even though names are not protectable under U.S. copyright laws. As a result, the younger Abdul-Jabbar had to change his jersey nameplate to simply "Abdul" while playing for the Dolphins. The football player had also been an athlete at UCLA.

Wikipedia

While in college in 1967 a roommate, George, and I crossed paths with Kareem. We were in a line to pay a driving ticket in Los Angeles. As we approached the window the women behind the counter kept looking over our heads at someone at the back of the line. They asked each other if the UCLA Bruins were playing that night.

After paying the fine we turned to leave. Looking back over the heads of those in line behind us my vision was blocked by a body towering over those in front of him. There stood the future leading scorer of the NBA who was still playing at UCLA at the time. He may be listed as seven feet tall but he looked like he was at least three feet taller than anyone before him in line. We left the building without thinking too much about the seeing Lew, one of the greatest players to have played the game of basketball.

In the tennis world a future star was emerging and someone who paid a steep price for being a gay athletic in her years as a pro. Sexism in sports was her cause and it came to a head when she played Bobby Riggs, a former champion in tennis who told the sports world women could never compete with men. Billie Jean King would forever be remembered for defeating Riggs and strengthening the role of women in sports.

Billie Jean King (*née* **Moffitt**; born November 22, 1943) is a former professional tennis player from the United States. She won 12 Grand Slam singles titles, 16 Grand Slam women's doubles titles, and 11 Grand Slam mixed doubles titles. King has been an advocate against sexism in sports and society. She won "The Battle of the Sexes" in 1973, in which she defeated Bobby Riggs, a former Wimbledon men's singles champion, for $100,000, winner take all.

King is the founder of the Women's Tennis Association, the Women's Sports Foundation, and owner of World Team Tennis, which was founded by her former husband, Larry King, Dennis Murphy, Frank Barman, and Jordan Kaiser.
Wikipedia

Battle of the Sexes
Main article: Battle of the Sexes (tennis)
Despite King's achievements at the world's biggest tennis tournaments, the U.S. public best remembers her for her win over Bobby Riggs in 1973, and winning $100,000 in the winner take all match.

Riggs had been a top men's player in the 1930's and 1940's in both the amateur and professional ranks. He won the Wimbledon men's singles title in 1939, and was considered the World No. 1 male tennis player for 1941, 1946, and 1947. He then became a self-described tennis "hustler" who played in promotional challenge matches. In 1973, he took on the role of male chauvinist. Claiming that the women's game was so inferior to the men's game that even a 55-year-old like himself could beat the current top female players, he challenged and defeated Margaret Court 6–2, 6–1. King, who previously had rejected challenges from Riggs, then accepted a lucrative financial offer to play him for $100,000, winner take all.

Dubbed the Battle of the Sexes, the Riggs-King match was played at the Houston Astrodome in Texas on September 20, 1973. The match garnered huge publicity. In front of 30,492 spectators and a worldwide television audience estimated at 50 million people in 37 countries, King beat Riggs 6–4, 6–3, 6–3. The match is considered a very significant event in developing greater recognition and respect for women's tennis (and perhaps women's sports in general). King said, "I thought it would set us back 50 years if I didn't win that match. It would ruin the women's [tennis] tour and affect all women's self-esteem."

In recent years, a persistent urban legend has arisen, particularly on the Internet, that the rules of tennis were modified for the match so that Riggs had only one serve for King's two and that King was allowed to hit into the doubles court area. In fact, the match was played under the normal rules of tennis. The legend is probably due to a mix-up between the King/Riggs match and one held years later between Jimmy Connors and Martina Navratilova, which featured the one serve/doubles alley rules.

In 2000, King received an award from the GLAAD, an organization devoted to reducing discrimination against gays, lesbians and bisexuals, for "furthering the visibility and inclusion of the community in her work." The award noted her involvement in production and the free distribution of educational films, as well as serving on the boards of several AIDS charities.
Wikipedia

Many athletes in the 60's who were gay did not come out due to the pressures of society. It was not until the 70's and 80's did the battle of sexual orientation become a giant issue and one that is still battled in the trenches of society and religion today.

Many black athletics converted to Islam during the 60's following the leadership of Ali and Kareem. These two were the best at what they did and their right to 'freedom of religion' during this period of change stood out as something America would have to deal with in the future.

Chapter Fifteen
A Shift in Religion and Beliefs

Many young adults like myself were brought up in one of the many different types of Christian religions found throughout North America. I was raised in the Presbyterian Church and attended the youth groups the church sponsored. I was never challenged with any fear based statements or interactions from any of the members of the Church. I enjoyed my upper middle class participation while memorizing bible verses when I was young and getting to know the cute girls who attended the high school youth gatherings each Sunday night.

The only difference I remember between religions was that which my mother tried to explain in her limited way. The other main church in the town of La Jolla was the Catholic Church and school with all their school age youth having to wear uniforms through the education years. The parents who wanted to make sure their children had a good education sent their kids to the nuns and priests for the Catholic way of making sure no one used their left hand when writing a school paper, and doing all those Hail Marys when they did something wrong.

Our family had several friends who were Catholic and they seemed just like any other kid our age. I even attended mass on occasion but understood little from the all Latin verses being read by the priest during this formal ritualistic approach to worshiping God in the early 60's. I have attended a Catholic service in recent years and have heard talks in English as well as women taking a part in the ceremonial service. Changes seem to be coming to this religious institution but slowly.

While in college I dated a Catholic girl whose father was even in training to become a priest at one time in his life. She was Irish and her father went on to become a postman for the government while raising seven children during the '60s. While we dated, Mary was a part of the underground movement in the Church who was attempting to change the way the old guard did things.

The Santa Barbara Mission was managed by Franciscan priests. They advocated modern music played on a guitar and they also sang the church songs in English. They believed priest should be able to get married and perform services in English. During the time I dated her she brought her Irish father to one of the services by the Franciscan priest. His belief in the old way of doing things did not allow him to enjoy this different way of worship. It took a few drinks after the service to calm him down.

I kept in touch with Mary for a few years before I left the country in 1970. She earned a teaching credential and joined the Peace Corps, spending time in Africa. I am sure the experience changed her life but she remained a Catholic girl to the end moving to Boston where the Kennedy clan and the Church held a strong grip on their believers. I am sure she married a man with her same Catholic beliefs as well.

While in college I had not attended any church services and was on a path of finding my connection with a higher power through other means. I was not satisfied with the cookie cutter approach to religion. I first started hearing about Eastern thought as other American youth started to travel to the east seeking gurus and starting Ashrams in America. The retreats taught meditation and other forms of spiritual practice used in ancient India and Southeast Asia. Hinduism, Buddhism and other sects of ancient practices of the East were attractive to the youth who wanted more than getting high on weed or being told they would go to hell by the traditional guilt religions of America.

The black community seemed to be engulfed in the Baptists beliefs of 'someday it would all get better' while many of their children found a break in the traditional beliefs of their parents by joining the Black Muslim movement brought over to America by Wallace Fard Muhammad and receiving attention when people like Malcolm X, Ali and Kareem made headlines by joining this religion years later.

Black Muslim movements
Main articles: Moorish Science Temple of America, Nation of Islam, American Society of Muslims, and The Nation of Gods and Earths

Malcolm X was the chief spokesman of the Nation of Islam. In 1964 he left the group and became a Sunni Muslim.

During the first half of the 20th century, a small number of African Americans established groups based on Islamic and Black supremacist teachings. The first of such groups created was the Moorish Science

Temple of America, founded by Timothy Drew (Drew Ali) in 1913. Drew taught that Black people were of Moorish origin but their Muslim identity was taken away through slavery and racial segregation, advocating the return to Islam of their Moorish ancestry.

The Nation of Islam (NOI) was the largest organization, created in 1930 by Wallace Fard Muhammad. It however taught a different form of Islam, promoting Black supremacy and labeling white people as "devils". Fard drew inspiration for NOI doctrines from those of Noble Drew Ali's Moorish Science Temple of America. He provided three main principles, which serve as the foundation of the NOI: "Allah is God, the white man is the devil and the so called Negroes are the Asiatic Black People, the cream of the planet earth". In 1934 Elijah Muhammad became the leader of the NOI, he deified Wallace Fard, saying that he was an incarnation of God, and taught that he was a prophet who had been taught directly by God in the form of Wallace Fard. Although Elijah's message caused great concern among White Americans, it was effective among Blacks attracting mainly poor people including students and professionals. One of the famous people to join the NOI was Malcolm X, who was the face of the NOI in the media.

Malcolm X was one of the most influential leaders of the NOI and advocated complete separation of blacks from whites. He left the NOI after being silenced for 90 days, he then formed his own black nationalist movement, and made the pilgrimage to Mecca, converting to Sunni Islam. He is viewed as the first person to start the movement among African Americans towards Sunni Islam.

W.D. Mohammed moved most of his followers into practicing orthodox Islam.

After the death of Elijah Muhammad, he was succeeded by his son, Warith Deen Mohammed. Mohammed rejected many teachings of his father, such as the divinity of Fard Muhammad and saw a white person as also a worshipper. As he took control of the organization he quickly brought in new reforms. He renamed it as the World Community of al-Islam in the West, later it became the American Society of Muslims. It was estimated that there were 200,000 followers of WD Mohammed at the time.

WD Mohammed introduced teachings which were based on orthodox Sunni Islam. He removed the chairs in temples, with mosques, teaching how to pray the *salah*, to observe the fasting of Ramadan, and to attend the pilgrimage to Mecca. It was the largest mass religious conversion in the 21st century, with thousands who had converted to orthodox Islam.

A small number of Black Muslims however rejected these new reforms brought by Imam Mohammed, Louis Farrakhan who broke away from the organization, re-established the Nation of Islam under the original Fardian doctrines, and remains its leader.

As of today it is estimated there are at least 20,000 members. However, today the group has a wide influence in the African American community. The first Million Man March took place in Washington, D.C. 1995 and was followed later by another one in 2000 which was smaller in size but more inclusive welcoming individuals other than just African American men The group sponsors cultural and academic education, economic independence, and personal and social responsibility.

The Nation of Islam has received a great deal of criticism for its anti-white, anti-Christian, and anti-semitic teachings, and is listed as a hate group by the Southern Poverty Law Center.
Wikipedia

My first introduction to meditation came from a college friend, Gary, who was studying psychology. There must have been a section on eastern religion he was covering in his studies because he introduced to me a technique of watching my breath in a dark room by my self in order to calm my mind and have better focus. I started to use this technique for about a week and found the practice rather soothing and calming. Without a teacher or anyone else to practice meditation with, I soon let it go and did not return to the technique again until years later when I traveled to India.

Zen is a school of Mahayana Buddhism and originated in China during the 6th century CE as Chán. From China, Zen spread south to Vietnam, to Korea and east to Japan.

The word *Zen* is derived from the Japanese pronunciation of the Middle Chinese word *Dzyen* (Modern Mandarin: *Chán*), which in turn is derived from the Sanskrit word *dhyāna*, which can be approximately translated as "absorption" or "meditative state".

Zen emphasizes the attainment of enlightenment and the personal expression of direct insight in the Buddhist teachings. As such, it de-emphasizes mere knowledge of sutras and doctrine and favors direct understanding through zazen and interaction with an accomplished teacher.

The teachings of Zen include various sources of Mahayana thought, especially Yogacara, the Tathagatagarbha Sutras and Huayan. The Prajnaparamita literature and, to a lesser extent, Madhyamaka have also been influential.

Zen in the Western world

Although it is difficult to trace when the West
first became aware of Zen as a distinct form
of Buddhism, the visit of Soyen Shaku, a
Japanese Zen monk, to Chicago during the
World Parliament of Religions in 1893 is
often pointed to as an event that enhanced its
profile in the Western world. It was during
the late 1950's and the early 1960's that the
number of Westerners, other than the
descendants of Asian immigrants, pursuing a
serious interest in Zen began to reach a
significant level. Especially Japanese Zen has
gained popularity in the West. The various
books on Zen by Reginald Horace Blyth, and
Alan Watts published between 1950 and
1975, contributed to this growing interest in
Zen in the West, as did the interest from beat
poets such as Jack Kerouac, Allen Ginsberg
and Gary Snyder.
Wikipedia

While in India from 1971 to 1975 I was
guided to attend a Buddhist meditation retreat
near Bombay in 1972. Vipassana became my
practice that helped me get in touch with the
higher power found in all religion, each using
a different name. Allah, God, Brahma,

Yahiya and Buddha are names used by humans in their attempt to give a label for this higher consciousness found in the universe. I have noticed that the newest religions, Christianity and Muslim, are two that do not recognize other religions as being valid or not the true religion as they claim they are. The newer religions are almost like young adolescent teens who still believe the world revolves around them and them only. They seem to believe they are the only ones who know the truth.

The 60's was also a time when the many gurus and holy men of India started to come to America. The Beatles were introduced to eastern thought through George Harrison when he became involved with Transcendentalism and Maharishi Mahesh Yogi. Donovan, Cat Stevens and a few other people from the music world found guidance through different Eastern religious practices. The shift in the way people in America found God was on. Zen became popular on the west coast and soon a change to eastern thought was on the rise with retreats and different approaches to the calming of one's self and focusing the mind.

Cat Stevens

Yusuf Islam (born **Steven Demetre Georgiou**, 21 July 1948), commonly known by his former stage name **Cat Stevens**, is a British singer-songwriter, multi-instrumentalist, educator, philanthropist, and prominent convert to Islam.

His early 1970's record albums *Tea for the Tillerman* and *Teaser and the Firecat* were both certified triple platinum in the United States by the RIAA. His 1972 album *Catch Bull at Four* sold half a million copies in the first two weeks of release alone and was *Billboard*'s number-one LP for three consecutive weeks. He has also earned two ASCAP songwriting awards in consecutive years for "The First Cut Is the Deepest", which has been a hit single for four different artists.

Stevens converted to Islam in December 1977 and adopted the name Yusuf Islam the following year. In 1979, he auctioned all his guitars for charity and left his music career to devote himself to educational and philanthropic causes in the Muslim community. He has been given several awards for his work in promoting peace in the world, including the 2003 World Award, the 2004 Man for Peace Award, and the 2007 Mediterranean Prize for Peace. In 2006, he returned to pop music with his first album of new pop songs in 28 years, entitled *An Other Cup*. He now goes professionally by the single name **Yusuf**. His most recent album, *Roadsinger*, was released on 5 May 2009. **Wikipedia**

Transcendental Meditation CAFÉ refers to the Transcendental Meditation technique, a specific form of mantra meditation, and to the Transcendental Meditation movement, a spiritual movement. The TM technique and TM movement were introduced in India in the mid-1950's by Maharishi Mahesh Yogi (1914–2008) and had reached global proportions by the 1960's.

The TM technique came out of and is based on Indian philosophy and the teachings of Krishna, the Buddha, and Shankara, as well as the Yoga Sutras of Patanjali, and is a version of a technique passed down from the Maharishi's teacher, Brahmananda Saraswati. The Maharishi also developed the Science of Creative Intelligence (SCI), a system of theoretical principles to underlie this meditation technique. Additional technologies were added to the Transcendental Meditation program, including "advanced techniques" such as the TM-Sidhi program (Yogic Flying).

TM is one of the most widely practiced, and among the most widely researched meditation techniques. Independent systematic reviews have not found health benefits for TM beyond relaxation or health education. Skeptics have called TM or its associated theories and technologies a pseudoscience.

In the 1950's, the Transcendental Meditation movement was presented as a religious organization. In 1977, the Transcendental Meditation technique was held to be a religion in a New Jersey court case. By the 1970's, the organization had shifted to a more scientific presentation while maintaining many religious elements in an attempt to appeal to the more secular West. Practitioners of Transcendental Meditation assert that their movement is not religious and describe it as a spiritual and scientific organization.

The TM movement has programs and holdings in multiple countries while as many as six million people have been trained in the TM technique, including The Beatles, Russell Brand, Oprah Winfrey and other well-known public figures. **Wikipedia**

It is now over 40 years since the influx of eastern religions and the different ways of worshipping came to America. Most are under attack by the conservative churches of this country. Freedom of religion was the cornerstone and the foundation of America but the old guard has now gone political. Anyone wanting to be a representative of the Republican Party had better be a conservative Christian and hold the same beliefs that they do which usually has nothing to do with the teachings of Christ. Such a thought process of trying to maintain the status quo is what drove many of the youth in the '60s to seek God on a spiritual plane instead of through the interpretations of the Religious Conservative beliefs.

Chapter Sixteen
Clothing and Dress Styles

Most of the clothing styles that came about during the '60s were on display in the Haight-Ashbury neighborhood of San Francisco. Clothing, along with the music and drug culture, was taking over the city. Head Shops sprung up everywhere selling all the needed items to be a 'flower child'. Many of the items sold in the shops were for inhaling grass or marijuana. These items came in the form of pipes, bongs, Indian hookahs or just plain Zig-Zag papers.

Haight-Ashbury

The mainstream media's coverage of hippie life in the Haight-Ashbury drew the attention of youth from all over America. Hunter S. Thompson labeled the district "Hashbury" in *The New York Times Magazine*, and the activities in the area were reported almost daily. The neighborhood's fame reached its peak as it became the haven for a number of the top psychedelic rock performers and groups of the time. Acts like Jefferson Airplane, the Grateful Dead and Janis Joplin all lived a short distance from the intersection. They not only immortalized the scene in song, but also knew many within the community as friends and family. Another well-known neighborhood presence was The Diggers, a local "community anarchist" group known for its street theatre who also provided free food to residents every day.

During the "Summer of Love", psychedelic rock music was entering the mainstream, receiving more and more commercial radio airplay. The Scott McKenzie song "San Francisco (Be Sure to Wear Flowers in Your Hair)," written by John Phillips of The Mamas & the Papas, became a hit single in 1967. The Monterey Pop Festival in June further cemented the status of psychedelic music as a part of mainstream culture and elevated local Haight bands such as the Grateful Dead, Big Brother and the Holding Company and Jefferson Airplane to national stardom. A July 7, 1967, *Time* magazine cover story on "The Hippies: Philosophy of a Subculture," an August CBS News television report on "The Hippie Temptation" and other major media interest in the hippie subculture exposed the Haight-Ashbury district to enormous national attention and popularized the counterculture movement across the country and around the world.

The Summer of Love attracted a wide range of people of various ages: teenagers and college students drawn by their peers and the allure of joining a cultural utopia; middle-class vacationers; and even partying military personnel from bases within driving distance.

The Haight-Ashbury could not accommodate this rapid influx of people, and the neighborhood scene quickly deteriorated. Overcrowding, homelessness, hunger, drug problems, and crime afflicted the neighborhood. Many people simply left in the fall to resume their college studies. On October 6, 1967, those remaining in the

Haight staged a mock funeral, "The Death of the Hippie" ceremony, to signal the end of the played-out scene. Mary Kasper explained the message of the mock funeral as follows:

We wanted to signal that this was the end of it, don't come out. Stay where you are! Bring the revolution to where you live. Don't come here because it's over and done with.
Wikipedia

Clothing started out with industrious people making their own styles of clothing. Loosely fitting open shirts and blouses, baggy pants, sandals and headscarves completed the wardrobe with the top models being Janis Joplin, Jimi Hendrix and Donovan. They brought the latest clothing styles to life every time they took the stage. Other music groups as well kept the fashion of bellbottoms and bright colors going and the Grateful Dead will always be remembered for their tie-dye tee shirts sold at their concerts and worn by the band.

The **Grateful Dead** was an American rock band formed in 1965 in Palo Alto, California. The band was known for its unique and eclectic style, which fused elements of rock, folk, bluegrass, blues, reggae, country, improvisational jazz, psychedelia, and space rock, and for live performances of long musical improvisation. "Their music," writes Lenny Kaye, "touches on ground that most other groups don't even know exists." These various influences were distilled into a diverse and psychedelic whole that made the Grateful Dead "the pioneering Godfathers of the jam band world."

They were ranked 57th in the issue *The Greatest Artists of all Time* by *Rolling Stone* magazine. They were inducted into the Rock and Roll Hall of Fame in 1994 and their Barton Hall Concert at Cornell University (May 8, 1977) was added to the Library of Congress's National Recording Registry.

The fans of the Grateful Dead, some of whom followed the band from concert to concert for years, are known as "Deadheads" and are known for their dedication to the band's music. From 2003 to 2009 former members of the Grateful Dead, along with other musicians, toured as The Dead and The Other Ones. There are many contemporary incarnations of the Dead, with the most

prominent touring acts being Furthur and Phil Lesh & Friends.
Wikipedia

My first pair of bell-bottom jeans were purchased while in college because the regular 501 Levi's were too hard to pull over my cowboy boots I wore at this time. I did not get too involved in the paisley shirts wardrobe but I made up for my lack of exploring the western attire by changing my entire clothing line while in India. Pajama pants, home spun cotton shirts and eastern style sandals is what I wore when I lived in India during the '70s.

Many of the styles made popular during the '60s began appearing in TV shows and movies as the entertainment industry attempted to keep up with the popular fads of the day. Movies and documentary films were made of the different music festivals including the Monterey Pop and Woodstock. They showed what the culture of the 'Turn on, Tune in and Drop out' wore while living and playing a part in this alternative life style.

Clothing styles of this culture continued into the '70s but by that time I have traveled to

Europe and was soon heading East by 1971. I read about the '70s from overseas but it was the '60s that set the tone for the many events that took place in the coming years.

Clothing Styles of the 60s
After designer Mary Quant introduced the mini-skirt in 1964, fashions of the '60s were changed forever. The mini skirt was eventually to be worn by nearly every stylish young female in the western world.

The mini dress was usually A-line in shape or a sleeveless shift. In 1964, French designer Andre Courreges introduced the "space look", with trouser suits, white boots, goggles, and box-shaped dresses whose skirts soared three inches above the knee. These were mainly designed in fluorescent colors and shiny fabrics such as PVC and sequins.

The leaders of mid-1960's style were the British. The Mods (short for Modernists) were characterized by their choice of style different from the 1950's and adopted new fads that would be imitated by many young people. As the Mods strongly influenced the fashion in London, 1960's fashion in general set the mode for the rest of the century as it became marketed mainly to young people. Mods formed their own way of life creating television shows and magazines that focused directly on the lifestyles of Mods. British rock bands such as The Who, The Small Faces, and The Kinks emerged from the Mod subculture.

The Mods were known for the Modern Jazz they listened to as they showed their new styles off at local cafes. They worked at the lower end of the work force, usually nine to five jobs leaving time for clothes, music, and clubbing. It was not until 1964 when the Modernists were truly recognized by the public that women really were accepted in the group. Girls had short, clean haircuts and often dressed in similar styles to the male Mods. The Mods' lifestyle and musical tastes were the exact opposite of their rival group known as the Rockers.The rockers liked 1950's rock-and roll, wore black leather jackets, greased, pompadour hairstyles, and rode motorbikes.

The look of the Mods was classy; they mimicked the clothing and hairstyles of high fashion designers in France and Italy; opting for tailored suits, which were topped by anoraks that became their trademark. They rode on scooters, usually Vespas or Lambrettas. The Mods dress style was often called the City Gent look. Shirts were slim, with a necessary button down collar accompanied by slim fitted pants. Levi's were the only type of jeans worn by Modernists. Flared trousers and bellbottoms led the way to the hippie stage introduced in the 1960's. Variations of polyester were worn along with acrylics.

Carnaby Street and Chelsea's Kings Road were virtual fashion parades. In 1966, the space age was gradually replaced by the Edwardian, with the men wearing double-breasted suits of crushed velvet or striped patterns, brocade waistcoats, shirts with frilled collars, and their hair worn below the collarbone. Rolling Stones guitarist Brian Jones epitomised this "dandified" look. Women were inspired by the top models of the day, which included Twiggy, Jean Shrimpton, Colleen Corby, Penelope Tree, and Veruschka. Velvet mini dresses with lace-collars and matching cuffs, wide tent dresses and culottes had pushed aside the geometric shift.

False eyelashes were in vogue, as was pale lipstick. Hemlines kept rising, and by 1968 they had reached well above mid-thigh. These were known as "micro-minis". This was when the "angel dress" made its appearance on the fashion scene. A micro-mini dress with a flared skirt and long, wide trumpet sleeves, it was usually worn with patterned tights, and was often made of crocheted lace, velvet, chiffon or sometimes cotton with a psychedelic print such as those designed by Emilio Pucci. The cowled-neck "monk dress" was another religion-inspired alternative; the cowl could be pulled up to be worn over the head. For evening wear, skimpy chiffon baby-doll dresses with spaghetti-straps were the mode as well as the "cocktail dress", which was a close-fitting sheath, usually covered in lace with matching long sleeves. Feather boas were occasionally worn.

In 1964, Bell-bottomed trousers were a new alternative to the capris of the early 1960's. They were usually worn with chiffon blouses, polo-necked ribbed sweaters or tops that bared the midriff.

The look of corsets, seamed tights, and skirts covering the knees had been abolished. The idea of buying urbanized clothing, which could be worn with separate pieces, was intriguing to women of this era in comparison to previously only buying specific outfits for certain occasions.

For daytime outerwear, short plastic raincoats, colorful swing coats and dyed fake-furs were popular for young women. In 1966, the Nehru jacket arrived on the fashion scene, and was worn by both sexes. Suits were very diverse in color but were for the first time ever fitted and very slimming. Waistlines for women were left unmarked and hemlines were getting shorter and shorter.

French actress Brigitte Bardot wearing a transparent top and a feather boa, 1968.

Footwear for women included low-heeled sandals and kitten-heeled pumps, as well as the trendy white go-go boots. Shoes, boots, and handbags were often made of patent leather or vinyl. The Beatles wore elastic-sided boots similar to Winkle-pickers with pointed toes and Cuban heels. These were known as "Beatle boots" and were widely copied by young men in Britain.

Late 1960's

Bell-bottoms, colorful headbands, and bare feet were part of the unisex hippie look that was popular in the late 1960's.

By 1968, the androgynous hippie look was in style. Both men and women wore frayed bell-bottomed jeans, tie-dyed shirts, work shirts, and headbands. Wearing sandals was also part of the hippie look for both men and women. Women would often go barefoot, and some went braless.

Fringed buckskin vests, flowing caftans, Mexican peasant blouses, gypsy-style skirts, scarves, and bangles were also worn by teenage girls and young women. Indian prints, batik and paisley were the fabrics preferred. For more conservative women, there were the "lounging" or "hostess" pajamas. These consisted of a tunic top over floor-length culottes, and were usually made of polyester or chiffon.

Another popular look for women and girls, which lasted well into the early 1970s, was the suede mini-skirt worn with a French polo-neck top, square-toed boots, and Newsboy cap or beret. Long maxi coats, often belted and lined in sheepskin, appeared at the close of the decade. Animal prints were also popular for women in the autumn and winter of 1969. Women's shirts often had transparent sleeves. Psychedelic prints, hemp and the

look of "Woodstock" came about in this generation.
Wikipedia

Chapter Seventeen
Sex and Marriage

Because I was in high school and college during most of the 60s, I admit that I was in the middle of raging hormones of a teenage male. Young men and women who were raised in strict God fearing conservative family environments were sent off to private bible colleges while the rest of us had to survive with our sexual urges in the public state college systems and universities. Those who did not go on to the higher learning institutions of life got jobs doing what they learned to do while in high school. Many in this last group married their girlfriends, became car mechanics, construction laborers or fishermen in my hometown of La Jolla. Many took over their parents' businesses or joined the army in order to find out what life had in store for them.

The Vietnam police action took the lives of a few high school friends at an early age. The army was the best job for a poor, unskilled young man of 18 years to go into and make a living. The military was the only choice for many young men in the '60s and for those who did survive, they learned discipline, and maybe a skill if they were something other than a foot soldier. The John Wayne movies of the '50s showing soldiers coming home as heroes' gave these young men with little prospects in the higher levels of the job market much to dream about. Being a war hero was a fulfilling direction to take if you believed that war was the answer to international problems.

The Sexual Revolution was a product of the '60s and the number one thing on most of the college population's minds was sex. Women were becoming more open with their physical relationships. Birth control, along with male contraceptives, made sex safer and user friendly. Playboy magazine saw its' peak with the nude pictorials and interesting articles many men claimed to be reading when their wives caught them with the publication in the bathrooms. High school boys had the latest edition of whatever skin magazine they could get their hands on, hidden under their mattress. Soon the number of sexually explicit reading material filled the liquor store newsstands and freedom of expression won out in the sex industry and became big business.

'Bob and Carol, Ted and Alice' was an example of Hollywood's attempt to accommodate the sexual experience being promoted by Hugh Hefner and his many articles about the open sexual experience. The fashion industry continued to make their renditions of what turns a man on in the undergarment department of women's apparel and eventually this transitioned into the bathing suit fashion with only the bare essentials being covered. The biggest change in the men's section of the same store was bikini underwear.

Hugh Hefner

Working as a copywriter for *Esquire*, he left in January 1952 after being denied a $5 raise. In 1953, he mortgaged his furniture, generating a bank loan of $600, and raised $8,000 from 45 investors — including $1,000 from his mother ("Not because she believed in the venture," he told *E!* in 2006, "but because she believed in her son.") — to launch *Playboy*, which was initially going to be called *Stag Party*. The undated first issue, published in December 1953, featured Marilyn Monroe from her 1949 nude calendar shoot and sold over 50,000 copies. (Hefner, who never met Monroe, bought the crypt next to hers at the Westwood Village Memorial Park Cemetery.

After it was rejected by *Esquire* magazine in 1955, Hefner agreed to publish in *Playboy* the Charles Beaumont science fiction short story, "The Crooked Man", about straight men being persecuted in a world where homosexuality was the norm. After receiving angry letters to the magazine, Hefner wrote a response to criticism where he said, "If it was wrong to persecute heterosexuals in a homosexual society then the reverse was wrong, too."

On June 4, 1963, Hefner was arrested for selling obscene literature after an issue of *Playboy* featuring nude shots of Jayne Mansfield was released. A jury was unable to reach a verdict.

His former secretary, Bobbie Arnstein, was found dead in a Chicago hotel room after an overdose of drugs in January 1975. Hefner called a press conference to allege that she had been driven to suicide by narcotics agents and federal officers. Hefner further claimed the government was out to get him because of *Playboy*'s philosophy and its advocacy of more liberal drug laws.

He has a star on the Hollywood Walk of Fame for television and has made several movie appearances as himself. In 2009, he received a "worst supporting actor" nomination for a Razzie award for his performance in *Miss March*.

A documentary by Brigitte Berman, *Hugh Hefner: Playboy, Activist and Rebel*, was released on July 30, 2010. He had previously granted full access to documentary filmmaker and television producer Kevin Burns for the A&E *Biography* special *Hugh Hefner: American Playboy* in 1996.

Hefner and Burns later collaborated on numerous other television projects, most notably on *The Girls Next Door*, a reality series that ran for six seasons (2005–2009) and 90 episodes.

In 1999, Hefner financed the Clara Bow documentary, *Discovering the It Girl*. "Nobody has what Clara had. She defined an era and made her mark on the nation," he stated.

Wickipedia

Bob & Carol & Ted & Alice is a 1969 comedy-drama film directed by Paul Mazursky. It stars Natalie Wood, Robert Culp, Elliott Gould and Dyan Cannon.

The screenplay was written by Paul Mazursky and Larry Tucker (who also produced the film). The original music score was composed by Quincy Jones. The original soundtrack album was released on Bell Records and featured Merrilee Rush performing a cover of the Burt Bacharach and Hal David's "What the World Needs Now Is Love" and Sarah Vaughan performing "I know that my Redeemer liveth" from Part III of Handel's *Messiah*. The cinematography for the film was by Charles Lang. It received four Academy Award nominations, including ones for Gould and Cannon.

The film was marketed with the tag line "Consider the possibilities."

After a weekend of emotional honesty at an Esalen-style retreat, Los Angeles sophisticates Bob and Carol Sanders (played by Robert Culp and Natalie Wood) return to their life determined to embrace free love and complete openness. Bob and Carol happily reveal their ensuing love affairs to everyone, sparking both the curiosity and repulsion of their more conservative close friends Ted and Alice Henderson (Elliott Gould and Dyan Cannon).

When the two couples travel together to Las Vegas, Ted admits to an affair of his own. An outraged Alice demands that this new ethos be taken to its obvious conclusion: a mate-sharing foursome. But when they are actually ready to begin the deed, something within all four of them prevents it; the film never explains what that something is or may be. In the last scene of the movie, they are in the elevator coming down from their "trip". They are shell shocked. All of them have woken up (in the evening) to their collective morning after. The music swells "...what the world needs now is love sweet love..."

Wikipedia

Most of the fraternity men I lived with during the two years I lived at the fraternity house had girlfriends with whom they slept on weekends at Motel 6 near the UCSB, or in their apartments after they moved out of the fraternity house their senior year. A few of the more daring actually got laid in the fraternity usually on a Saturday night when a lot of alcohol was involved and a toga garment could easily be removed. Safe sex was a requirement at this time and birth control was used. The pill was a big part of keeping pregnancy at a distance.

Sex in America had been suppressed since the country's founding and the arrival of the white man. Puritans and Quakers were among the first who built towns and cities in America. Many of the religious leaders of such groups seemed disgusted with the human body. Sheets were hung between a man and a woman in some sects and the sexual act was performed through a hole in the sheet. Touching the bare flesh was kept to a minimum and the fear of God punishing a person for having sexual thoughts was constantly on their minds.

Sex was still treated like something few people participated in during the 50's and TV was a perfect example of how it was portrayed to the public. All the family shows had the parents sleeping in separate beds including 'Leave It To Beaver' and 'I Love Lucy.' It was a wonder the population in America even grew based on the sexual practices shown on TV.

Europe had a different approach to sex and did not seem as uptight regarding the experience at all. I lived in Salzburg, Austria from 1963 to 1964 and found out the city had a government controlled red light district. All cities of any size had such a district. It was easier to monitor the sexual act, tax it and make sure diseases were not transmitted. This approach made more sense instead of trying to suppress the industry.

The European Continent was considered a barbarian place where ungodly people did ungodly things according to the uptight religious rights groups in the '60s. The foundations of all that sexual suppression began to shake and crumble when freedom of speech and expression took the country by storm. Women without bras and wearing mini skirts were just the beginning of the sexual pendulum swinging to the left. Wife swapping parties became the choice of the 'jet set' and America seemed to be going through a period of seeking a balance between the sexual suppression of the past and the sexual revolution of the '60s.

Divorce in America was on the rise. In the late 50's my parents divorced and I was treated as an outcast of society because they were no longer together. By the '60s I was not alone. Other young adults had parents who divorced. I even knew a parent from the Catholic Church who faced excommunication because of her status as a divorcee. The church in Italy did not accept the concept of adults marrying and then going their separate ways. This institution has been slow in many ways when it comes to meeting the needs of society. I was amazed the Catholic Church finally made the change in the mass services by speaking in the language of the people instead of Latin. 'Full disclosure' as to what the priests were actually saying was a big leap in this institution.

The hippie movement led the way in the Sexual Revolution and 'free love' became the catch phrase of the day. I suppose the term referred to the other alternative, which was to pay for love. Parties and 'love ins' were held and John Lennon stayed in bed with Yoko Ono for a week or so, in order to emphasize the expression 'Make Love, Not War.' Sex was in the mainstream of news. With the heightened feelings that came with the smoking of marijuana, everyone seemed to be enjoying themselves. Those who went to bible colleges and were told God would punish them for expressing themselves sexually may not have experienced the Sexual Revolution at all. Wow, I believe I dodged a bullet there.

Free Love

The modern consensus is that the sexual revolution in 1960's America was typified by a dramatic shift in traditional values related to sex, and sexuality. Sex became more socially acceptable outside the strict boundaries of heterosexual marriage.

Studies have shown that, between 1965 and 1975, the number of women who had had sexual intercourse prior to marriage showed a marked increase. The social and political climate of the 1960's was unique; one in which traditional values were often challenged loudly by a vocal minority.

The various areas of society clamoring for change included the Civil Rights movement, (see SCLC and SNCC) the 'New Left', and women, with various women's rights organizations appearing in the latter years of the decade in particular. This climate of change led many, particularly the young, to challenge social norms.

With the success that the Civil Rights movement was having, others who wanted change knew that the time was ripe for them to bring it about. The combination of liberal government, general economic prosperity, and the ever present threat of nuclear annihilation marked the 1960's apart from any decade that had come before it, and whilst conservatism was by no means dead, liberalism enjoyed a widespread revival, which helped to facilitate the climate in which the 'sexual revolution' took place. Indeed, Lyndon Johnson was the first acting president to endorse birth control, a hugely important factor in the change of American sexual attitudes in the 1960's.

The Pill

"The pill" provided many women a more affordable way to avoid pregnancy. Before the pill was introduced many women did not look for long term jobs. Previously, the typical women would jump out of the job market when she got impregnated and would reenter it when her child was of school attending age.

Abortion was too expensive and there were too many health risks involved. We can see a trend in the increasing age of women at first marriage in the decades between 1930-1970 after contraception was provided to non-married females. As part of the woman's quiet sexual revolution, pills gave women control over their future. In a way, the ability to pursue higher education without the thought of pregnancy, gave women more equality in educational attainment. Since women could have a choice to use birth control to finish their education, a higher percentage graduated from school and college ultimately gaining professional careers.

This was due in part to fears over illegitimate pregnancy and childbirth, and social (particularly religious) qualms about contraceptive, which was often seen to be 'messy' and unchristian. Modernization and secularization helped to change these attitudes, and the first oral contraception was developed in 1951 partly due to Women's Rights campaigner Margaret Sanger who raised $150,000 to fund its development.

While the Pill eventually came to be seen as a symbol of the Sexual revolution, its origins stem less from issues of women's sexual liberation and more from 1960's political agendas. In the early 1960's, President Lyndon Johnson instituted his social reform policy, The Great Society, which aimed to eliminate poverty and racial injustice.

During this time, the Pill was endorsed and distributed by doctors as a form of population control to counter the fear of over population, which coincided with President Johnson's goal to eliminate poverty. By 1960, the Food and Drug Administration had licensed the drug. 'The Pill', as it came to be known, was extraordinarily popular, and despite worries over possible side effects, by 1962, an estimated 1,187,000 women were using it.

The pill divorced contraception from the act of intercourse itself, making it more socially acceptable, and easier to tolerate for many detractors than other types of contraception (which had been around for years).

Heralded as a technological marvel, the pill was a trusted product of science in an increasingly technological age, and was heralded as one of man's 'triumphs' over nature. It was often said that with the invention of the pill, the women who took it had immediately been given a new freedom - the freedom to use their bodies as they saw fit, without having to worry about the burden of unwanted pregnancy.

It was also not the case that the pill went completely unopposed. The Pill became an extremely controversial subject as Americans struggled with their thoughts on sexual morality, controlling population growth and women's control of their reproductive rights. Even by 1965, birth control was illegal in some US states, including Connecticut and New York.

Campaigns by people like Estelle Griswold went all the way to the US Supreme Court, where on June 7, 1965 it was ruled that under the First Amendment, it was not the business of the government to dictate the usage of contraception by married couples. Unmarried women who requested gynecological exams and oral contraceptives were often denied or lectured on sexual morality. Those women who were denied access to the Pill often had to visit several doctors before one would prescribe it to them. In 1972, a further ruling in *Baird* extended that right to unmarried couples.

Women's rights movements also heralded the pill as a method of granting women sexual liberation, and saw the popularity of the drug as just one signifier of the increasing desire for equality (sexual or otherwise) amongst American women. The pill and the sexual revolution was therefore an important part of the drive for sexual equality in the 1960's.

As a consequence, the pill and the sexual freedom it provided to women are frequently blamed for what many believe are regressions in quality of life. Since the sexual revolution, out-of-wedlock births, sexually transmitted diseases, teen pregnancy, and divorce have all risen considerably. Since the '60s, marriage

has declined by a 1/3 and divorce has doubled. During the 1960's there were only four big STDs, now there are twenty-four. Since the sexual revolution, children living in single-parent families has tripled.
Wikipedia

Combined oral contraceptive pill

Combined oral contraceptive pill (COCP)

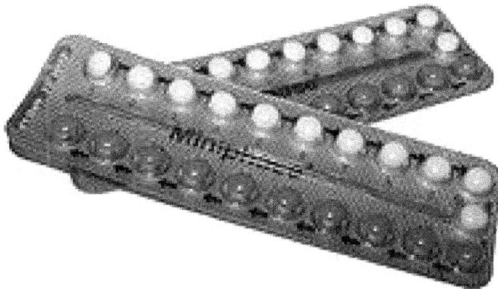

Background

Birth control type	Hormonal
First use	?

Failure rates (first year)

Perfect use	0.3%

Typical use	8%

Usage

Duration effect	1–4 days
Reversibility	Yes
User reminders	Taken within same 24-hour window each day
Clinic review	6 months

Advantages and disadvantages

STD protection	No
Periods	Regulates, and often lighter and less painful
Weight	No proven effect
Benefits	Reduced ovarian and endometrial cancer risks. May treat acne, PCOS, PMDD, endometriosis
Risks	possible small increase in some

cancers, Small
reversible increase
in DVTs; Stroke,
Cardio-vascular
disease

Medical notes

Affected by the antibiotic rifampin,
the herb Hypericum (St. Johns Wort)
and some anti-epileptics, also
vomiting or diarrhea. Caution if
history of migraines.

The **combined oral contraceptive pill**
(**COCP**), often referred to as the **birth-
control pill** or colloquially as "**the Pill**", is a
birth control method that includes a
combination of an estrogen (oestrogen) and a
progestin (progestogen). When taken by
mouth every day, these pills inhibit female
fertility. They were first approved for
contraceptive use in the United States in
1960, and are a very popular form of birth
control. They are currently used by more than
100 million women worldwide and by almost
12 million women in the United States. Usage
varies widely by country, age, education, and
marital status: one third of women aged 16–
49 in the United Kingdom currently use either

the combined pill or a progestogen-only "minipill", compared to only 1% of women in Japan.
Wikipedia

Chapter Eighteen
News and the Media

I was just listening to a radio show on Public Radio called "Wait, Wait, Don't Tell Me." I get the show sent to me through my email in Mexico because I do not have a receiver that can pick up the show as it is broadcast. One of the scenarios used to try and stump the listener was about a TV nightly news station. They were tired of all gimmicks the different news teams were using to try and get people interested in their news coverage program. The morning news shows brought the audience everything from dressing the TV anchors in costumes for the holiday or an event that was happening at the time, to cooking classes or the latest fat reducing program out there in the world of overweight Americans. All this extra stuff was used to fill the two-hour slot for the morning show. It really was not news at all.

The made up story was as follows. The TV station decided to fire all the news people and hire new ones who looked like the news anchors of the '60s such as Edward R. Morrell, and Walter Cronkite. These were the big names in the '60s news programs. The news also was changed to black and white during the broadcast and presented the stories just like they were broadcast in the '60s. Only stories or current events in the world were covered and the news anchors, who looked like those anchormen during '60s, could even smoke while giving the world the information to the public, just as they did 45 to 50 years before.

Even though the scenario was fabricated and not the correct answer, it was the one that this listener chose to be true. His reasoning was that because he was only 27 he wanted to find out more about the '60s. He thought that watching how the news was presented during that time would be interesting to himself and others in his age group.

I believe the reader can now see why I decided to write such a book even though much of the information comes from the

Internet. The events of the '60s can now be accessed in one paperback or eBook and those interested in reading about this powerful time of change in America can do so. I do admit this is a brief and limited presentation of this vast period of change. but it is a start. I also do not hold back on my more liberal views as I talk about the '60s so the reader will have to weed through my slant on things if they hold a more conservative outlook on life.

James Michener, had he chosen this topic in the '70s or '80s, would have given this era an in-depth coverage with the help of all the researchers he used to write his other books. I am retired and living in Mexico. The internet is what I have to use to present the subject along with my personal life during this time frame. I hope it gives the reader, who did not live during this period, some insight into what happened and why your parents or grandparents are the way they are today.

The news in the '60s compared to the news of today has changed much like the service stations from the same time period and the service stations of today. In the 60's gas stations only sold gas, oil and tires and did car repairs in the stations. They also cleaned your windshield, checked your oil level and air pressure in your tires and collected your money from your car window. Today one can do all their junk food shopping and maybe get a loaf of bread and a gallon of milk at a gas station. No tires are sold and there is no one who can work on your car if needed. Workers at the gas stations of today make sure the donut shelves are full and reorder all the chips and soft drinks needed to keep the traveler happy.

Customers fill their own gas tanks and check the air pressure in their tires. They even wash their own windows of the car and if they have a credit card they never have to have any contact with the person operating the station sitting behind the cash register. They just swipe the card before they fill up and be on their way. America is doing its best to depersonalize business transactions for the sake of speed and profit. "Time is Money" became the poster of America in the 70's and the theme continues on into the 21st century.

The news networks of the '60s did one thing. They gave the news and only the news. They did not fill the airwaves with unnecessary information and try to control the way people thought about politics, gay marriage, economy, and immigration. Fox news and CNN seem to have both of those left and right views covered today. The '60s presented the news to the world as it broke and allowed the viewers to make up their own minds about a story.

Edward R. Morrell did make a stand during the McCarthy era and fought against the slanted views of those trying scare tactics to support their extreme views. Several stations on TV and the radio, like McCarthy, use these same tactics today and seem to be successful in 'fooling some of the people all of the time.' Many personalities on the radio are multi-millionaires because they have a large audience who hang onto every word they say. To me they are the McCarthy's of the present era of the information age.

Walter Leland Cronkite, Jr. (November 4, 1916 – July 17, 2009) was an American broadcast journalist, best known as anchorman for the *CBS Evening News* for 19 years (1962–81). During the heyday of *CBS News* in the 1960's and 1970's, he was often cited as "the most trusted man in America" after being so named in an opinion poll. Although he reported many events from 1937 to 1981, including bombing in World War II, the Nuremberg trials, combat in the Vietnam War, Watergate, the Iran Hostage Crisis, and the murders of President John F. Kennedy, civil rights pioneer Martin Luther King, Jr., and The Beatles musician John Lennon, he was known for extensive TV coverage of the U.S. space program, from Project Mercury to the Moon landings to the Space Shuttle. He was the only non-NASA recipient of a Moon-rock award. Cronkite is well known for his departing catchphrase "*And that's the way it is,*" followed by the date on which the appearance is aired.

Cronkite reported on location during the Vietnam War.

In mid-February 1968, on the urging of his executive producer Ernest Leiser, Cronkite and Leiser journeyed to Vietnam to cover the aftermath of the Tet Offensive. They were invited to dine with General Creighton Abrams, the current commander of all forces in Vietnam, whom Cronkite knew from World War II. According to Leiser, Abrams told Cronkite, "we cannot win this Goddamned war, and we ought to find a dignified way out."

Upon return, Cronkite and Leiser wrote separate editorial reports based on that trip. Cronkite, an excellent writer, preferred Leiser's text over his own. On February 27, 1968, Cronkite closed "Report from Vietnam: Who, What, When, Where, Why?" with that editorial report:

We have been too often disappointed by the optimism of the American leaders, both in Vietnam and Washington, to have faith any longer in the silver linings they find in the darkest clouds. They may be right, that Hanoi's winter-spring offensive has been forced by the Communist realization that they could not win the longer war of attrition, and that the Communists hope that any success in the offensive will improve their position for eventual negotiations. It would improve their position, and it would also require our realization, that we should have had all along, that any negotiations must be that -- negotiations, not the dictation of peace terms. For it seems now more certain than ever that the bloody experience of Vietnam is to end in a stalemate.

This summer's almost certain standoff will either end in real give-and-take negotiations or terrible escalation; and for every means we have to escalate, the enemy can match us, and that applies to invasion of the North, the use of nuclear weapons, or the mere commitment of one hundred, or two hundred, or three hundred thousand more American troops to the battle. And with each escalation, the world comes closer to the brink of cosmic disaster. To say that we are closer to victory today is to believe, in the face of the evidence, the optimists who have been wrong in the past. To suggest we are on the edge of defeat is to yield to unreasonable pessimism. To say that we are mired in stalemate seems the only realistic, yet unsatisfactory, conclusion.

On the off chance that military and political analysts are right, in the next few months we must test the enemy's intentions, in case this is indeed his last big gasp before negotiations. But it is increasingly clear to this reporter that the only rational way out then will be to negotiate, not as victors, but as an honorable people who lived up to their pledge to defend democracy, and did the best they could.

Following Cronkite's editorial report, President Lyndon Johnson is reported to have said, "If I've lost Cronkite, I've lost Middle America." This account has been questioned in a recent publication on journalistic accuracy. Several weeks later, Johnson announced he would not seek reelection.

During the 1968 Democratic National Convention in Chicago, Cronkite was anchoring the CBS network coverage as violence and protests occurred outside the convention, as well as scuffles inside the convention hall. When Dan Rather was punched to the floor (on camera) by security personnel, Cronkite commented, "I think we've got a bunch of thugs here, Dan."
Wikipedia

Edward Roscoe Murrow, KBE (born **Egbert Roscoe Murrow**; April 25, 1908 – April 27, 1965) was an American broadcast journalist. He first came to prominence with a series of radio news broadcasts during World War II, which were followed by millions of listeners in the United States and Canada.

Fellow journalists Eric Sevareid, Ed Bliss, and Alexander Kendrick considered Murrow one of journalism's greatest figures, noting his honesty and integrity in delivering the news.

A pioneer of television news broadcasting, Murrow produced a series of TV news reports that helped lead to the censure of Senator Joseph McCarthy.

Criticism of McCarthyism

See It Now focused on a number of controversial issues in the 1950's, but it is best remembered as the show that criticized McCarthyism and the Red Scare, contributing if not leading to the political downfall of Senator Joseph McCarthy.

On March 9, 1954, Murrow, Friendly, and their news team produced a half-hour *See It Now* special entitled "A Report on Senator Joseph McCarthy". Murrow used excerpts from McCarthy's own speeches and proclamations to criticize the senator and point out episodes where he had contradicted himself. Murrow and Friendly paid for their own newspaper advertisement for the program; they were not allowed to use CBS's money for the publicity campaign or even use the CBS logo.

Nevertheless, the broadcast contributed to a nationwide backlash against McCarthy and is seen as a turning point in the history of television. It provoked tens of thousands of letters, telegrams, and phone calls to CBS headquarters, running 15 to 1 in favor. In a retrospective produced for *Biography*, Friendly noted how truck drivers pulled up to Murrow on the street in subsequent days and shouted "Good show, Ed. Good show, Ed."

Murrow offered McCarthy a chance to appear on *See It Now* to respond to the criticism. McCarthy accepted the invitation and made his appearance three weeks later, but his rebuttal served only to further decrease his already fading popularity.

In the program following McCarthy's appearance, Murrow commented that the senator had "made no reference to any statements of fact that we made" and contested the personal attacks made by "the junior senator from Wisconsin" against himself.

Wikipedia

Joseph Raymond "Joe" McCarthy
(November 14, 1908 – May 2, 1957) was an
American politician who served as a
Republican U.S. Senator from the state of
Wisconsin from 1947 until his death in 1957.
Beginning in 1950, McCarthy became the
most visible public face of a period in which
Cold War tensions fueled fears of widespread
Communist subversion. He was noted for
making claims that there were large numbers
of Communists and Soviet spies and
sympathizers inside the United States federal
government and elsewhere. Ultimately,
McCarthy's tactics and his inability to
substantiate his claims led him to be censured
by the United States Senate.

The term *McCarthyism,* coined in 1950 in
reference to McCarthy's practices, was soon
applied to similar anti-communist activities.
Today the term is used more generally in
reference to demagogic, reckless, and
unsubstantiated accusations, as well as public
attacks on the character and/or patriotism of
political opponents.

Born and raised on a Wisconsin farm,
McCarthy earned a law degree at Marquette

University in 1935 and was elected as a circuit judge in 1939, the youngest in state history. At age 33, McCarthy volunteered for the United States Marine Corps and served during World War II. He successfully ran for the United States Senate in 1946, defeating Robert M. La Follette, Jr. After three largely undistinguished years in the Senate, McCarthy rose suddenly to national fame in February 1950 when he asserted in a speech that he had a list of "members of the Communist Party and members of a spy ring" who were employed in the State Department.

McCarthy was never able to prove his sensational charge.

In succeeding years, McCarthy made additional accusations of Communist infiltration into the State Department, the administration of President Harry S. Truman, Voice of America, and the United States Army. He also used charges of communism, communist sympathies, or disloyalty to attack a number of politicians and other individuals inside and outside of government.

With the highly publicized Army–McCarthy hearings of 1954, McCarthy's support and popularity began to fade. On December 2, 1954, the Senate voted to censure Senator McCarthy by a vote of 67 to 22, making him one of the few senators ever to be disciplined in this fashion. McCarthy died in Bethesda Naval Hospital on May 2, 1957, at the age of 48. The official cause of death was acute hepatitis; it is widely accepted that this was caused, or at least exacerbated, by alcoholism. **Wikipedia**

Besides the new coverage of the Vietnam conflict and the Cuban Missile crisis, the landing on the moon had to be the one big positive item that came out of the 60s. When the first man walked on the moon it became one of those moments when everyone seemed to know what they were doing at the time. Many were watching the event on TV.

Nasa and the moon landing.

A total of twelve men have landed on the Moon. This was accomplished with two US pilot-astronauts flying a Lunar Module on each of six NASA missions across a 41-month time span starting on 21 July 1969 UTC, with Neil Armstrong and Buzz Aldrin on Apollo 11, and ending on 14 December

1972 UTC with Gene Cernan and Jack Schmitt on Apollo 17 (with Cernan being the last to step off the lunar surface).

All Apollo lunar missions had a third crew member who remained on board the Command Module. The last three missions had a rover for increased mobility.

Scientific background

In order to go to the moon, a spacecraft must first leave the gravity well of the Earth. The only practical way of accomplishing this currently is with a rocket. Unlike other airborne vehicles such as balloons or jets, a rocket is the only known form of propulsion which can continue to increase its speed at high altitudes in the vacuum outside the Earth's atmosphere.

Upon approach of the target moon, a spacecraft will be drawn ever closer to its surface at increasing speeds due to gravity. In order to land intact, a spacecraft must either be ruggedized to withstand a "hard landing" impact of less than about 100 miles per hour (160 km/h) (not possible with human occupants), or it must decelerate enough for a "soft landing" with negligible speed at contact. The first three attempts by the Americans to perform a successful hard moon landing with a ruggedized seismometer package in 1962 all failed.

The Soviets first achieved the milestone of a hard lunar landing with a ruggedized camera in 1966, followed only months later by the first unmanned soft lunar landing by the Americans. The escape velocity of the target moon is roughly equivalent to the speed of a crash landing on its surface, and thus is the total velocity which must be shed from the target moon's gravitational attraction for a soft landing to occur. For Earth's Moon, this figure is 2.38 kilometers per second (1.48 mi/s).

Such a change in velocity (referred to as a delta-v) is usually provided by a landing rocket, which must be carried into space by the original launch vehicle as part of the overall spacecraft. An exception is the soft moon landing on Titan carried out by the Huygens probe in 2005. As the only moon with an atmosphere, landings on Titan may be accomplished by using atmospheric entry techniques that are generally lighter in weight than a rocket with equivalent capability.

The Soviets succeeded in making the first crash landing on the Moon in 1959. Crash landings may occur because of malfunctions in a spacecraft, or they can be deliberately arranged for vehicles which do not have an on board landing rocket. There have been many such moon crashes, often with their flight path controlled to impact at precise locations on the lunar surface. For example, during the Apollo program the S-IVB third stage of the Saturn V moon rocket as well as the spent ascent stage of the lunar module were deliberately crashed on the Moon several times to provide impacts registering as a moonquake on seismometers that had been left on the lunar surface. Such crashes were instrumental in mapping the internal structure of the Moon.

To return to earth, the escape velocity of the moon must be overcome for the spacecraft to escape the gravity well of the moon. Rockets must be used to leave the Moon and return to space. Upon reaching Earth, atmospheric entry techniques are used to absorb the kinetic energy of a returning spacecraft and reduce its speed for safe landing. These functions greatly complicate a moon landing mission and lead to many additional operational considerations.

Any moon departure rocket must first be carried to the Moon's surface by a moon landing rocket, increasing the latter's required size. The moon departure rocket, larger moon landing rocket and any Earth atmosphere entry equipment such as heat shields and parachutes must in turn be lifted by the original launch vehicle, greatly increasing its size by a significant and almost prohibitive degree. This necessitates optimizing the sizing of stages in the launch vehicle as well as consideration of using space rendezvous between multiple spacecraft.
Wikipedia

Chapter 19
Education, the Elephant
In the Room

Since I spent most of the 60's either in high school or college and eventually went on to become a teacher for twenty-five years, I have some strong feelings as to what has happened in the past forty or fifty years to the education system in America. In the community of La Jolla, CA where I grew up, public schools, a Catholic school and a few private schools made up the system of learning. The Catholic and private schools had to wear uniforms and the public system did not.

The nuns were the teachers of the Catholic schools and in the 60's I was told there were no left-handed students in this system because writing with the left hand was the sign of the devil. This rumor may have been spread by anyone who was not a Catholic in La Jolla. Rulers were used to smack the hands of those reverting back to their natural way of writing (left handed) and I believe the corporal punishment system was still in play for those acting out students that needed discipline to control their behavior. Horror stories reached the ears of the public school students and just seeing a nun walking down the sidewalk caused some kids to cross over to the other side of the street just to be sure they would not get a smack.

Wealthy families sent their children to either the private or Catholic schools in order to protect them from the common masses attending the public schools. Some of the wildest high school girls I remember went to Sacred Heart in La Jolla. I have often wondered why there are strip acts in which the women dress up in Catholic school uniforms to perform their entertainment dances. Was it because these young Catholic girls had parents who were trying to protect them from the awakening of their sexuality? A few of these girls showed up at many of the wild high school parties at large homes when the parents were vacationing in Scottsdale, AZ or Hawaii? Some of these Catholic girls were the ones who were the real "Wild Ones". That was the reputation a few of these young Catholic ladies in La Jolla had in the '60s.

One or two private schools were established for those students who either excelled in scholastics and the parents wanted them to continue to exceed or for the few, like my neighbor, who had learning disabilities and needed extra help in school. The public system did not have special education like they do now. Those students who had disabilities and could not go to a private school were thrown into the mix with the rest of the population and the regular teachers had to do their best to make sure the special needs students learned what they could without any special help.

The rest of the students grew up together in the elementary, Junior High and High School system going through all the pains of being teenagers and somehow surviving. La Jolla was a conservative town made up of wealthy families who were either members of The Beach and Tennis Club or the La Jolla Country Club. The other half were the poorer middle class who just happened to live and work in La Jolla and mingle with the wealthy kids who went to the local high school.

The poorer students who came from lower income families, usually tried to excel in sports if they had any abilities at all. This worked for a few black athletics gifted in basketball, football and track.

There were also the typical auto and woodshop students who may have come from families with means but did not have the academic abilities or the support of the home to do well in the field of scholarly achievement. They were usually the troublemakers and made the vice principal earn his salary by having to monitor their behavior and come down on them when fighting and alcohol mixed into the school environment.

Drugs were not a part of the early '60s environment in La Jolla but alcohol did play a major part in the acting out of students from this small coastal town. One student I grew up with became an alcoholic by his senior year and he had to down a couple of beers in the bushes near the school before he could face the pressures of being in an academic environment he cared little for.

Those students that excelled in the high school environment, either academically or through athletics, joined all the clubs and student organizations. They helped the teachers and administrators maintain a level a level of normality in the school. Those who felt they did not fit usually slipped through the cracks or started jobs after school to prepare them for the minimum wage occupations waiting for them after graduation.

Several girls I knew trained to be beauty store employees and were working twenty hours a week during the school years and full time in the summer. A few young men were learning the lobster trade and would set their cages before school started. They brought in the catch at 3 pm when the academic day ended. Many went on to become full time fishermen in their adult lives.

After graduation I was given the opportunity to go to Europe for the summer and broaden my perspective of the world. I resisted this opportunity at first because I felt I was in work heaven selling burgers two blocks from the beach where I spent my off hours surfing whenever the waves were good. I eventually conceded to take the graduation gift from my mother and the chance to fly in a 707, the big jet airliner of the day, all the way to a foreign country.

My summer was spent touring Germany, France and Austria. I even attempted to learn German in the city of Salzburg in the country of Austria. I eventually had the opportunity to live a year in Salzburg with four other American girls from the tour who also decided to stay and expand their worldly education.

Two of the girls were sent by their parents in the hope that the separation from the wild life of parties in La Jolla High would ground them and help them to grow up. Both were well on their way to becoming alcoholics. Sending them to a country where the drinking age was 15 did not seem to me as a solution for changing their behavior. I think the parents had no control over their daughters. Alcohol was not considered a danger in the '60s so sending them to live with a strict Austrian family was their attempt to change their behavior and ready them for adulthood.

The other two girls lived with another Austrian family. One of them eventually married the oldest son and moved back to the states. Years later after she divorced I found she was remarried and lived in a Midwest state surrounded by cornfields and football.

During my stay in Salzburg I attended an all boys school and found out a lot about the education system in Europe. I lived with a family that had two daughters. One daughter, Sonia, was motivated to do well in school and used me whenever she needed help with English. The other daughter, Monica, was on track to learn a trade. She did eventually enter into the beauty and hair maintenance profession at age 13 when she could not pass the proficiency test allowing her to pursue a higher level of education.

Sonja loved school and chose to continue her education with the possibility of a better paying job after school was finished.

In Europe the school system is more practical in recognizing those young adults who have the aptitude to pursue higher education versus those who would rather learn a trade or skill in the work force. The trade schools gave them the knowledge and skills needed in their life instead of being forced to learn about world history or higher math concepts, which they had no desire to learn.

When a young adult does go into the 'Trade School' program in Europe they still attend classes but study those subjects that have to do with the profession they are learning. Math has to be learned in most of the building professions. The ability to read and create blueprints and 'measure twice and cut once' are important skills as a builder. Many of the businesses in the area where I lived in Salzburg hired these young adults and used them to complete the work needed in order to satisfy the customer.

A car mechanic shop was located on my walk to the bus from the house where I lived. The owner divided the young men into four different levels of skill depending upon the year and age each student was in the program. For instance the first year students were paid a minimal wage and did the menial tasks of setting up the shop, keeping it clean during the day and sweeping it out at night. They probably ran errands for the owner and learned some basic skills in the auto business. First year apprentices were kept in line by the older students so any horsing around by a 13 or 14 year old, while on the job, was minimal at the most.

The 2nd year students had more advanced duties and were also paid more. By the fourth year the 17 or 18-year-old students were doing all the advanced mechanical duties needed to work on cars. They were usually the second in command under the boss or another skilled mechanic who may have worked in the garage. Upon graduation the young men had a skill and a diploma allowing them to work almost anywhere in Europe.

In the 60s the best cars made were either German or English. I noticed the foreign car shops in America had many German mechanics working on them and they also had a reputation of being the best car technicians in America. The reason for this fact had to do with this simple truth. These workers started learning their trade from age 13 and were skilled as a mechanic by 17 or 18.

The closest thing I remember to a trade school in La Jolla was the one-hour wood shop, metal shop or auto shop classes available for those students who took an interest in using their hands in a work related profession. These students were not interested in learning about the Roman Empire and being able to answer obscure questions on Jeopardy having to do with topics ranging from authors or scientific discoveries to words ending in 'ing'. Do not get me wrong about those who are skilled in such a vast array of subjects. I love watching this program but 98 or 99 percent of the population could never make the cut to get onto this show and would have to try out for the other half hour game show based on luck and how well one could piece together a word after buying all the vowels in the alphabet and solving the puzzle.

By the time this book is published Vanna and Pat may have finally retired and who knows who will take over after they are gone. They are now in their 30th year together.

The other part of the education puzzle I have noticed in America is this: because we do not have classes set up for students who do not have the drive or aptitude for higher education, they are still forced to attend an institution that offers nothing for them to use in real life. Instead, many of these students come to classes, act out and are some of the biggest troublemakers in a system that does not offer anything they want or need. Drugs are sold in the school parking lot and fights occur on the school grounds.

The public education system has lost control of the students and does not remove those individuals who disrupt the learning of those who want to be in this system. The troublemakers are placed in containment rooms and monitored by aides because the schools are only paid if the student is at the institution for the duration of the day.

Teachers are constantly breaking up fights by these students who are forced to attend an institution that holds no future for them and their interests.

The parents and other educators who are tired of this out of control system have found out how to start their own schools and still have the state pay for the education with state funds. Charter schools are springing up everywhere. Some are good and some disguise their religious agendas under the Charter school banner.

I worked in two charter schools after I retired as a teacher in 2008 and recognized one main difference in both organizations that separated them from the public domain. In the two years at a high school charter institute I saw no fights at all in the school. Ninety percent of the students were there to get an education. Academics was their main goal. The other ten percent were there because their parents placed them there hoping they would develop the drive needed to go on to college or higher learning. Two students were expelled because of drug connections and selling to other students.

The only ones who left the charter school to go to a public school were the good athletes. They had hopes of winning a scholarship to a college through a sport in which they excelled. Eighty percent of the students went on to higher education and most could look back at high school as being a positive experience where they were safe and could be who they were without the fear of being picked on or bullied.

One of the students I met at the charter school in Flagstaff saw nothing of value in the classes he was forced to learn about because his interest lay in the field of being a motorcycle mechanic. He wanted to open his own shop but had to spend six hours a day in a school he hated and doing schoolwork that held little or no value to him at all. He was a round peg being forced to fit into a square hole and the education experience was not a positive one for him.

My 25 years of teaching lay in the Special Education System that was trying to force different shaped pegs into that same square hole. Most of my students never had or would ever have the ability to learn, retain and use the information being forced upon them in the system of education in the states today or even in the '60s. The top-heavy administration had no answers for these problems and it seems they were mostly concerned with maintaining order during their watch and reach retirement without too much flack or "shit hitting the fan".

As long as the school system in the states continues to use the one size fits all approach to educating our youth, disruptions, acting out and killings will occur in these places where we continue to place disgruntled youth with little or no interest in the slots in which they are being forced to squeeze. I support the charter school attempts to give their youth a good education and put boundaries around behavior and acting out. A closer monitoring of such schools who try to push their religious agendas while receiving public funding needs to be addressed but other than that I do not see public schools surviving in their approach to education and preparing the youth for tomorrow.

Those with academic ability will attend a charter school and what is left is the angry youth who use violence and acting out to get what they want. The teachers in public schools have to put up with managing these war zones. Many teachers are there only to survive for another year until they can either retire or call it quits and go into another work sector like a prison guard at a jail where they would be safer.

This is my rant and rave regarding schools today. Wake up America. Columbine may be the first big shock but I predict more to come. The angry youth who do not fit into the mold of football, cheerleading and learning the social skills attached to the artificial life of high school act out in ways where the end result is suicide or shooting sprees taking out those students who made their lives miserable.

The skills for those who do not care about education as it is forced upon them today are available in the many tech schools upon graduation from high school. In Europe this approach is available at a much earlier age and the result is an 18 year old with the ability to earn a living vs. an 18 years old in the states who may go on to flipping burgers or clerking in a mall and never learn a trade where they can earn a decent living. The military is another option for those who earn their diploma.

I do not expect to see the Education system admitting they were wrong and turn towards the program that works in Europe. What I do see are Charter Schools increasing in numbers. Parents are making attempts to keep their children safe and have an education. The public high schools could become the trade schools of the future and bring back the shop classes and subjects needed for the work force. Computer skills and areas of technology are being taught to students out of high school and these ITT institutes are increasing in numbers all the time.

For those who did survive the high school education of the '60s and went on to higher education, here is what was happening in those institutions.

The Free Speech Movement in higher education
1966–1970

The Free Speech Movement had long-lasting effects at the Berkeley campus and was a pivotal moment for the civil liberties movement in The Sixties. It was seen as the beginning of the famous student activism that existed on the campus in the 1960's, and continues to a lesser degree today. There was a substantial voter backlash against the players involved in the Free Speech Movement. Ronald Reagan won an unexpected victory in the fall of 1966 and was elected Governor; The newly elected governor directed the UC Board of Regents to dismiss UC President Clark Kerr because of the perception that he had been too soft on the protesters. The FBI had kept a secret file on Kerr.

Reagan had gained political traction by campaigning on a platform to "clean up the mess at Berkeley". In the minds of those involved in the backlash, a wide variety of protests and a wide variety of concerned citizens and activists were lumped together.

Furthermore, television news and documentary filmmaking had made it possible to photograph and broadcast moving images of protest activity. Much of this media is available today as part of the permanent collection of the Bancroft Library at

Berkeley, including iconic photographs of the protest activity by student Ron Enfield (then chief photographer for the Berkeley campus newspaper, the Daily Cal). A reproduction of what may be considered the most recognizable and iconic photograph of the movement, a shot of suit-clad students carrying the Free Speech banner through the University's Sather Gate in the Fall of 1964, now stands at the entrance to the college's Free Speech Movement Café.

Earlier protests against the House Committee on Un-American Activities meeting in San Francisco in 1960 had included an iconic scene as protesters were literally washed down the steps inside the Rotunda of San Francisco City Hall with fire hoses. The conservative film *Operation Abolition*, which depicted this scene, became an organizing tool for the protesters.
Wikipedia

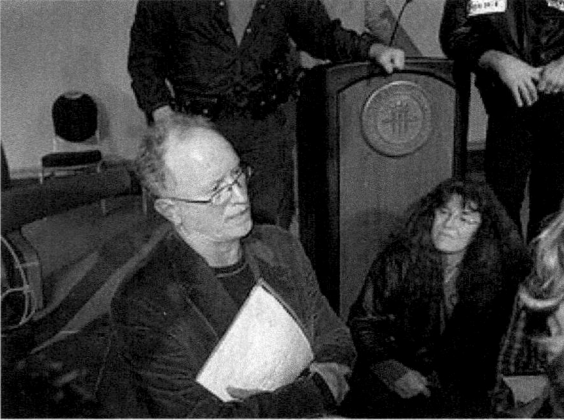

Ayers speaks to audience members following a forum on education reform.

William Charles "Bill" Ayers (born December 26, 1944) is an American elementary education theorist and a former leader in the movement that opposed U.S. involvement in the Vietnam War. He is known for his 1960's activism as well as his current work in education reform, curriculum, and instruction. In 1969 he co-founded the Weather Underground, a self-described communist revolutionary group that conducted a campaign of bombing public buildings during the 1960's and 1970's, in response to U.S. involvement in the Vietnam War.

He is a retired professor in the College of Education at the University of Illinois at Chicago, formerly holding the titles of Distinguished Professor of Education and Senior University Scholar. During the 2008 US presidential campaign, a controversy arose over his contacts with then-candidate Barack Obama. He is married to Bernardine Dohrn, who was also a leader in the Weather organization.
Wikipedia

A few other names appeared during this time and were related to the free speech movement of the '60s. Abby Hoffman and the Chicago Seven were just a few of the many people that appeared in the headlines either speaking out against the war in Vietnam or for the downfall of American Society. I started to pull myself away from the idea of using violence to get the wanted results. By the end of the '60s I was planning on living in Europe, away from the U.S. and its' ideas of war as a means of getting what they needed to survive.

Abbot Howard "Abbie" Hoffman
(November 30, 1936 – April 12, 1989) was a

political and social activist who co-founded the Youth International Party ("Yippies").

Hoffman was arrested and tried for conspiracy and inciting to riot as a result of his role in protests that led to violent confrontations with police during the 1968 Democratic National Convention, along with Jerry Rubin, David Dellinger, Tom Hayden, Rennie Davis, John Froines, Lee Weiner and Bobby Seale. The group was known collectively as the "Chicago Eight"; when Seale's prosecution was separated from the others, they became known as the Chicago Seven. While the defendants were initially convicted of intent to incite a riot, the verdicts were overturned on appeal.

Hoffman came to prominence in the 1960's, and continued practicing his activism in the 1970's, and has remained a symbol of the youth rebellion of that era.
Wikipedia

The **Chicago Seven** (originally **Chicago Eight**, also **Conspiracy Eight/Conspiracy Seven**) were seven defendants—Abbie Hoffman, Jerry Rubin, David Dellinger, Tom Hayden, Rennie Davis, John Froines, and Lee

Weiner—charged with conspiracy, inciting to riot, and other charges related to protests that took place in Chicago, Illinois on the occasion of the 1968 Democratic National Convention. Bobby Seale, the eighth man charged, had his trial severed during the proceedings, lowering the number from eight to seven.

Wikipedia

While having the book edited by a friend name Bill I was asked why I didn't have anything in the story regarding the SDS. Since I left the country in 1970 I couldn't remember all the organizations but I do remember this one.   Here is what Wikipedia had to say about this organization.

Students for a Democratic Society (SDS) was a student activist movement in the United States that was one of the main representations of the country's New Left. The organization developed and expanded rapidly in the mid-1960's before dissolving at its last convention in 1969. SDS has been an important influence on student organizing in the decades since its collapse. Participatory democracy, direct action, radicalism, student power, shoestring budgets, and its organizational structure are all present in varying degrees in current American student activist groups. Though various organizations have been formed in subsequent years as proposed national networks for left-wing student organizing, none has approached the scale of SDS, and most have lasted a few years at best.

A new incarnation of SDS was founded in 2006.

Wikipedia

Chapter 20
Surfing and the X Games

Music, drugs, and the Vietnam police action were influential upon this era. If I were black, the civil right's movement would make the top three of the most important aspects of the 60s. If I were a woman, Gloria Steinem would be my poster child. A young man joining the army would have to say the Vietnam conflict was their choice as the most influential aspect that marked their life during this time. What I didn't write much about but what I enjoyed the most was surfing and how it changed during this period of time. The audience for surfing was limited to those who lived near water that had waves to ride. In the '60s the sport spread like a tidal wave or tsunami and even reached India in the '70s due to a fellow traveler named Parker. He brought a surfboard to the land of spirituality and both he and I caught some waves in the day and meditated in the evenings. (Living Beneath the Radar)

Surfing can now be found in almost every country today that has waves. I have seen surfers on tidal swells going up rivers in jungle areas of the world and even riding swells made from glaciers crashing into Arctic waters of Alaska. Of all the seven continents, only Antarctica does not seem to have any surfers catching any swells in the frigid waters to the south. The other six continents all have surfers doing their thing in some capacity. South Africa; France and Portugal in Europe; Indonesia in Asia; Brazil in South America; both coasts in North America and of course, the shark infested waters of Australia are the main countries participating in this sport.

Pontiac woodie, used by early surfers

Surf culture includes the people, language, fashion and life surrounding the art and sport of surfing.

The history of surfing began with the ancient Polynesians. That initial culture directly influenced modern surfing which began to flourish and evolve in the early 20th century, with popularity spiking greatly during the 1950's and 1960's, principally in Hawaii, Australia, and California. It continues to progress and spread throughout the world. It has at times affected popular fashion, music, literature, films, jargon, and more.

The fickle nature of weather and the ocean, plus the great desire for the best possible types of waves for surfing, make surfers dependent on weather conditions that may change rapidly. *Surfer Magazine*, founded in the 1960's when surfing had gained popularity with teenagers, used to say that if they were hard at work and someone yelled "Surf's up!" the office would suddenly be empty. Also, since surfing has a restricted geographical necessity (i.e. the coast), the culture of beach life often influenced surfers and vice versa. Localism or territorialism is a part of the development of surf culture in which individuals or groups of surfers designate certain key surfing spots as their own.

Aspects of 1960's surf culture in Southern California, where it was first popularized, include the woodie, bikinis and other beach wear, such as boardshorts or baggies, and surf music. Surfers developed the skateboard to be able to "surf" on land; and a number of other boardsports. Of these the most popular being snowboarding and skateboarding, in addition

to other spin-offs that have grown out of the sport ever since.
Wikipedia

Surfers and spectators in boats at Mavericks, a world-renowned big wave break a half mile off the coast of Half Moon Bay, California

Big Wave culture

A surfer in Santa Cruz, California

Big Wave Surfing

A non-competitive adventure activity involving riding the biggest waves possible (known as "rhino hunting") is also popular with some surfers. A practice popularized in the 1990's has seen big wave surfing revolutionized, as surfers use personal watercraft to tow them out to a position where they can catch previously un-ride able waves (see tow-in surfing). These waves were previously un-rideable due to the speed at which they travel. Some waves reach speeds of over 60 km/h; personal watercraft enable surfers to reach the speed of the wave thereby making them rideable.

Personal watercraft also allows surfers to survive wipeouts. In many instances surfers would not survive the battering of the "sets" (groups of waves together). This spectacular activity is extremely popular with television crews, but because such waves rarely occur in heavily populated regions, and usually only a very long way out to sea on outer reefs, few spectators see such events directly.

Though surfers come from all walks of life, the basis of the beach bum stereotype comes from that great enthusiasm that surfers can have for their sport. Dedication and perfectionism are also qualities that surfers bring to what many have traditionally regarded as a commitment to a lifestyle as well as a sport.

For specific surf spots, the state of the ocean tide can play a significant role in the quality of waves or hazards of surfing there. Tidal variations vary greatly among the various global surfing regions, and the effect the tide has on specific spots can vary greatly among the spots within each area. Locations such as Bali, Panama, and Ireland experience 2-3 meter tide fluctuations, whereas in Hawaii the difference between high and low tide is typically less than one meter.

Each surf break is different, since the underwater topography of one place is unlike any other. At beach breaks, the sandbanks can change shape from week to week, so it takes commitment to get good waves (a skill dubbed "broceanography" by a few California surfers[).

The saying "You should have been here yesterday," became a commonly used phrase for bad conditions. Nowadays, however, surf forecasting is aided by advances in information technology, whereby mathematical modeling graphically depicts the size and direction of swells moving around the globe.

The quest for perfect surf has given rise to a field of tourism based on the surfing adventure. Yacht charters and surf camps offer surfers access to the high quality surf found in remote, tropical locations, where trade winds ensure offshore conditions.

Along with the rarity of what surfers consider truly perfect surf conditions (due to changing weather and surf condition) and the inevitable hunt for great waves, surfers often become dedicated to their sport in a way that precludes a more traditional life. Surfing instead, becomes their lifestyle.

The goals of those who practice the sport vary, but throughout its history, many have seen surfing as more than a sport, as an opportunity to harness the waves and to relax and forget about their daily routines. Surfers have veered from even this beaten path, and foregone the traditional goals of first world culture in the hunt for a continual 'stoke', harmony with life, their surfing, and the ocean. They; these "Soul Surfers", are a vibrant and long-standing sub-group. Competitive surf culture, centered around surf contests and endorsement deals, and localism's disturbance of the peace, are often seen in opposition to this.

The historic surf village of Ocean Beach, San Diego, California, is a good example of a place devoted to the surfing lifestyle, having been introduced originally by OB Lifeguard George Freeth.
Wikipedia

Modern surfing

Around the beginning of the 20th century, Hawaiians living close to Waikiki began to revive surfing, and soon re-established surfing as a sport. Duke Kahanamoku, "Ambassador of Aloha," Olympic medalist, and avid waterman, helped expose surfing to the world.

Kahanamoku's role was later memorialized by a 2002 first class letter rate postage stamp of the United States Postal Service. Author Jack London wrote about the sport after having attempted surfing on his visit to the islands. Surfing progressed tremendously in the 20th century, through innovations in board design and ever increasing public exposure.

Surfing's development and culture was centered primarily in three locations: Hawaii, Australia, and California, although the first footage of surfing in the UK was in 1929 by Louis Rosenberg and a number of friends after being fascinated by watching some Australian surfers. However it was only in the 1960s when it truly became worldwide and the release of the film Gidget boosted the sport's popularity immensely, moving surfing from an underground culture into a national fad and packing many surf breaks with sudden and previously unheard of crowds.

B-movies and surf music such as the Beach Boys and Surfaris based on surfing and Southern California beach culture (Beach Party films) as it exploded, formed most of the world's first ideas of surfing and surfers. This conception was revised again in the 1980's, with newer mainstream portrayals of surfers represented by characters like Jeff Spicoli from *Fast Times at Ridgemont High.* **Wikipedia**

Surfing Today
The anonymous sleeve notes on the 1962 album "Surfin' Safari", the first album to be released on the Capitol label by The Beach Boys, include a rather tongue-in-cheek description of the sport of surfing thus: 'For those not familiar with the latest craze to invade the sun-drenched Pacific coast of Southern California, here is a definition of "surfing" - a water sport in which the participant stands on a floating slab of wood, resembling an ironing board in both size and shape, and attempts to remain perpendicular while being hurtled toward the shore at a rather frightening rate of speed on the crest of

a huge wave (especially recommended for teen-agers and all others without the slightest regard for either life or limb)'.

Regardless of its usually erroneous portrayal in the media, true surfing culture continued to evolve quietly by itself, changing decade by decade. From the 1960's fad years to the creation and evolution of the short board in the late '60s and early '70s to the performance hotdogging of the neon-drenched 1980's and the epic professional surfing of the 1990's (typified by Kelly Slater, the "Michael Jordan of Surfing").
Wikipedia

The rise of different sports came about in the '60s and today there are the X Games that support everything from skateboards, dirt bikes, motor cross, and trick bikes on huge ramps risking life and limb to do what they love. Skydiving, hang gliding and other air sports came a little later and the world of thrill seekers continues to create new ways to get a rush.

I would like to add a chapter with more internet information quoting a product and a man of the '60s. Yogi Berra. He was famous for his baseball skills and his one-liners. One of the most famous statements was,

"It's **Déjà vu** all over again."

Déjà vu, from French, literally "already seen", is the phenomenon of having the strong sensation that an event or experience currently being experienced has been experienced in the past. **Wikipedia**

Chapter 21
Yogi Berra

Lawrence Peter "Yogi" Berra (born May 12, 1925) is a former American Major League Baseball catcher, outfielder, and manager. He played almost his entire 19-year baseball career (1946–1965) for the New York Yankees. Berra was one of only four players to be named the Most Valuable Player of the American League three times and is one of only six managers to lead both American and National League teams to the World Series. As a player, coach, or manager, Berra appeared in 21 World Series. He was elected to the Baseball Hall of Fame in 1972.

Berra is widely regarded as one of the greatest catchers in baseball history. According to the win shares formula developed by sabermetrician Bill James, Berra is the greatest catcher of all time and the 52nd greatest non-pitching player in major-league history.

Berra, who quit school after the eighth grade, has a tendency toward malapropism and fracturing the English language. "It ain't over till it's over" is arguably his most famous example, often quoted. Simultaneously denying and confirming his reputation, Berra once stated, "I really didn't say everything I said."
Wikipedia

Yogi Berra in 1956.

Yogi became almost as famous for his quotes as he did as a catcher and manager for the NY Yankees. Books have been written about his famous lines and I believe the '60s can expand upon what he had to say.

"You can observe a lot by watching."
There was so much going on in the '60s that watching was all that many of us could do. News coverage on TV was getting better and every night a generation of Americans were settling in front of the 'boob tube' with their Swanson's TV dinners that had a taste of aluminum in every bite and watching Walter

Cronkite and other personalities tell it like it was.

TV seemed to have a lot to do with spreading the feeling of not being safe in the world. Violence in the news made up the main stories and people were afraid to go out of their homes because they were being exposed to the insanity of the world in their own living room. Before TV became popular in the '50s people resided on their front porch and visited neighbors walking by as they sat on their swings. They knew everyone in the area where they lived, what their kids were doing and the names of most of the people on their block.

In the '60s house designs changed and life turned to the backyards and private areas of the house where no one could watch the neighbors go by. No one knew the person three doors down from them and if they came to your door you may not even recognize them. Yogi was right. You can observe a lot by watching and when the population of the '60s and '70s stopped watching, no one knew what was going on in the neighborhood. Only the violence in their town on the TV gave them unnecessary information and kept them in a state of fear.

"The future ain't what it used to be." Another great quote by Yogi really put the '60s into its' rightful place in time. The '50s was "Leave it to Beaver", "I Love Lucy" and simple shows portraying a simple life. "Ozzie and Harriet" was one of the best of these shows because it cast their son, Ricky, breaking from the mold of his parents and brother and getting into music with rock and roll. He became a star and would have lasted a little longer if he did not start using crack cocaine and light his plane on fire. "Come on Baby Light My Fire" was not a tribute to Ricky.

Eric Hilliard Nelson (May 8, 1940 – December 31, 1985), better known as **Ricky Nelson** or **Rick Nelson**, was an American singer-songwriter, instrumentalist, and actor. He placed 53 songs on the Billboard Hot 100 between 1957 and 1973 including "Poor Little Fool", which holds the distinction of being the first #1 song on Billboard magazine's then newly created Hot 100 chart. He recorded nineteen additional top-ten hits, and was inducted into the Rock and Roll Hall of Fame on January 21, 1987.

Nelson began his entertainment career in 1949 playing himself in the radio sitcom series, *The Adventures of Ozzie and Harriet*, and, in 1952, appeared in his first feature film, *Here Come the Nelsons*. In 1957, he recorded his first single, debuted as a singer on the television version of the sitcom, and recorded a number one album, *Ricky*. In 1958, Nelson recorded his first number one single, "Poor Little Fool", and, in 1959, received a Golden Globe Most Promising Male Newcomer nomination after starring in the western film, *Rio Bravo*. A few films followed, and, when the television series was cancelled in 1966, Nelson made occasional appearances as a guest star on various television programs.

Nelson and Sharon Kristin Harmon were married on April 20, 1963, and divorced in December 1982. They had four children: Tracy Kristine, twin sons Gunnar Eric and Matthew Gray, and Sam Hilliard. On February 14, 1981, a son (Eric Crewe) was born to Nelson and Georgeann Crewe. A blood test in 1985 confirmed Nelson was the child's father. Nelson was engaged to Helen Blair at the time of his death in an airplane crash on December 31, 1985.

In 1996, Ricky Nelson was ranked #49 on TV Guide's 50 Greatest TV Stars of All Time. **Wikipedia**

The '60s was nothing like the '50s so Yogi again had it right. The future ain't what it used to be.

"If the world were perfect, it wouldn't be. " This quote is actually quite spiritual. Each of us on earth has an image of what the world would look like if we could create it our way. Different religious sects practice certain beliefs and try to define the world according to their views. Go to another group and they see the world differently than the first group. Violence or non-violence seems to be two choices in life. This belief or view is among the countless possibilities present for the individual to choose from or they need to make up their own.

The '60s was a time of shaking up the views of America and showing that there are many different ways to see almost everything. I have my way of seeing the world based on my experiences and influences. Others have their experiences and they are different than yours or mine. We are heading into a different future and each of us is living that life based on our beliefs. This difference is what we grew up with in life and it will continue to change because change is the one constant that is true for all of us. How we adapt to change is the challenge. Fighting change leads to anger and mental melt down. Staying centered in who we are and what we believe and allowing the universe to flow in this thing called change, keeps us sane and removes us from fear of the unknown. We are safe if we believe it is so.

"When you come to a fork in the road....Take it." This last quote by Yogi, to me, is the best one of all. We go through life and we are presented with choices as to which direction we should take. Parents and other adults try to direct their kids in a direction based on their belief systems and what molded them into who they are. Some parents try to live through their children and guide them towards the goals in life that they never reached. Happiness is everyone's goal and such general comments such as "If only he or she would do this or that, they would be happy" is a perfect example of how many of us think. These same individuals want others to live and believe the same as they do. Then the world would be much happier.

I have always challenged my parents and their goals they had for me in life. Each of us has a reason we are living here on earth and if we do not make our own choices or take our own personal forks in the road, we are not learning much about why we are here on earth. Take the fork in the road and let your inner voice guide you to wherever it leads you. There are no mistakes. There is only indecision that holds you back.

I lived the '60s and survived. I made life choices and I have no regrets. Stop where you are and take a look around. "It doesn't get any better than this" can be a mantra for you.

If you want something better then "stop doing the same thing over and over again and expecting a different outcome." That is the definition for insanity.

When someone comes up to you and says they have the secret to life, tell them to keep it or it will not be a secret any longer. We all have the capacity to find what we need in life but we first have to learn to listen. It is within us and not out there in the loud world telling us "How white our shirts could be" and "he can't be a man because he doesn't smoke the same cigarettes as me." Satisfaction is a goal and the guy on the commercials is doing his best to give you that end result based on whatever he is selling.

Oh, I just saw the curtain move. I wonder what the wizard is thinking of trying to sell us now?

Chapter 22
Reunions and Looking Back

As I start to wind down this book and head into 2013 I am faced with the prospect of my 50th high school reunion in August of 2013. I have thought about it for a while and I now live within driving distance of making this affair a reality. At the same time I really have no interest in conversations centered around

"What have you been doing for the past 50 years?" We were all products of the '60s.

Many classmates went into the military and served in Vietnam while others got jobs and worked for companies for 30 or 40 years, staying in or around our hometown of La Jolla. Many will show up displaying their riches in the form of nice cars or tailored suits and showing off their botox wives and selves in their attempt to ward off the inevitable in their search for happiness. I have a few high school friends on Facebook and several have told me I need to go to the reunion. These are the ones who still live in town and never really left. Their lives are what they are but not filled with many experiences outside the realm of our hometown. My living in Mexico is alien to them and usually their fear-based stories reach me. Their conclusion is, "Mexico is unsafe."

I have often wondered if they watch the same news I watch from Mexico. The violence surrounding them in America is spreading and "the right to bear arms" in America plays a big part of the reason for this violence. Murders in all the major cities occur on a daily basis and those watching this news coverage have become numb to this nightly occurrence.

I really do not have a desire to go and pretend to be interested in what others I have not seen in 50 years have to say. I suspect they would not be that interested in what I have to say as well. The reader may think this sounds self-centered but it is not. To pretend to be interested in the life of someone you may have known fifty years ago but have not seen since is about as phony as one can be. Many that go to these gatherings either go every year because they want to try and relive the glory days of their youth or to show off what living the American dream has brought them in the form of material goods. Remember, the goal in Capitalism is, "whoever has the most in the end wins."

College was my formative years and traveling around the world for nearly a decade was my education. Living in the '60s directed me to my fork in the road and I took it. Trying to share my life at a dinner with other individuals wrapped up in their own worlds would be humorous at best.

This brings me to a conclusion of this short summary of the era that changed many lives in America and influenced how they see the world. I have done my best to present to the reader, who was not involved in the '60s, a glimpse of the excitement and turmoil that happened.

Today we are in another period of turmoil and direction changing events leading up to the elections in 2012 and beyond. The Mayan calendar has some people believing the end of the world would happen in the month of December of 2012. By the time the book is published the election will be over and the consequences will be in play. Also the Mayan calendar predictions will have been proven as true or not. I have my views of what I want to see happen and at the same time I have released any expectations of how the outcomes will affect me, and my life on earth, for the remaining years.

I am sure many of my comments throughout the book are not in line with many who lived during this amazing time and I am sure there are many stories about the '60s that have already been written. More will appear in movies as stories are shared in their attempts to explain this time in America. It was a time when I realized there were other humans out in the world trying to control how I thought and acted. It was also a time when the famous quote by Helen Keller became so very true. "Life is either a daring adventure, or nothing at all."

Helen Adams Keller (June 27, 1880 – June 1, 1968) was an American author, political activist, and lecturer. She was the first deaf blind person to earn a Bachelor of Arts degree. The story of how Keller's teacher, Anne Sullivan, broke through the isolation imposed by a near complete lack of language, allowing the girl to blossom as she learned to communicate, has become widely known through the dramatic depictions of the play and film *The Miracle Worker*.

A prolific author, Keller was well-traveled, and was outspoken in her anti-war convictions. A member of the Socialist Party of America and the Industrial Workers of the World, she campaigned for women's suffrage, labor rights, socialism, and other radical left causes. She was inducted into the Alabama Women's Hall of Fame in 1971. **Wikipedia**

Chapter 23
Where Are We Today?

The '60s played out as a tumultuous time period with a vast amount of information available for those who either lived it or went through the motions during this time. It seemed to be a period where many people began to question the 'Good ole Boy's' way of doing things and keeping the status quo to 'we do not want to keep doing it that way and so we are making a stand for something new.' If you watched the elections in 2012 there is a similar message here that separates the two main parties.

Progress has always been made that way. Columbus knew the world was not flat. Galileo figured out the world was not the center of the universe. A couple of brothers brought man into the era of flight. The list in the '60s with the changes in diet, music, drug use, religion, civil rights, woman's liberation, war, news and information are just a few of the many shifts that took place. People did not seem to just follow the path of those who went before them but instead blazed their own trail.

Today I see the U.S. as polarized between beliefs as it has ever been in my lifetime. The 'good ole boy's' belief system is still in place and to me this represents a resistance to change. When things are going just fine for a few, those who are benefitting from keeping things the same do not want to upset the applecart. The wealthy in America are determined to stay that way and anything that comes along that interferes with that formula cannot be allowed to exist. These individuals represent the man behind the curtain in the "Wizard of OZ" and they are doing their best to present an illusion of what the population wants.

Paying higher taxes because one has a large income is outrageous to a person who has six or seven houses, on his third marriage and probably has a drinking problem. Why should he have to pay more so his factory workers have good medical coverage or a livable wage.

The polarization of America is evident in the recent events since 2007. The economic melt down due to a non-regulated financial market and housing market were the big players. The financial industry with all the money scared the American government into believing they were too big to fail. The Republicans conducted the first bail out and the Democrats did the second one after electing a black president. Financial collapse was so close to happening and instead of joining forces to fix the problem, divided America used the situation to blame each other for the situation.

The Tea Party started soon after America finally broke the race barrier for a president and pretended to be against this administration because of high taxes. We were in a financial melt down and they wanted to lower taxes, continue to give the rich a tax break and try to fix the country by downsizing the biggest economy in the world.

The Democrats and their resistance to any downsizing while continuing to give money to the Auto industry and other financial institutions seemed to be a completely different direction than what the Republicans wanted. Instead of concessions, open warfare took place in the house and the senate. Huge gains by the Democrats in 2008 were lost and the government went into another do nothing mode in 2010 led by the Tea Party and their wins in many states.

The people of America began their protest against the financial system with marches across the country in 2011. The sit in and live in movement reminded me of a resurgence of the marches and protests of the '60s. The only thing that stopped the protest was winter. Since the biggest financial body is in NY and winter does exist with low temperatures, I can hardy wait until spring comes around and the protests start all over again.

As much as I can remember with the help of Wikipedia, I have attempted to give a short summary of this period of time in our modern history. Being retired and living in Mexico, most of the residents from the States have their own personal experiences of the '60s and may see it differently. Many were busy raising children and just getting by as they started out in their different careers in life. Many were in school either college or high school and everyone has a tale to tell regarding the '60s and what it meant to them.

The attempt of this book to share this time with others too young to know much about the '60s and have a somewhat broader interpretation than that of their parents or uncle who lived in this era. I used Wikipedia for a particular reason. It is the only informational encyclopedia that is constantly changing and being updated as new information comes in. Some people do not like Wikipedia and what it stands for and may not believe the things they read in this book. If you do not like the way the '60s is interpreted in this book then here is a suggestion. Write you own. The state of Texas is attempting to do so with history because they do not like Thomas Jefferson's insights into the separation of 'Church and State' and are attempting to rewrite our history. Keep an eye on this development and the people attempting to do this in Texas.

Thomas Jefferson and Religion

Jefferson rejected the orthodox Christianity of his day and was especially hostile to the Catholic Church as he saw it operate in France. Throughout his life Jefferson was intensely interested in theology, biblical study, and morality. As a landowner he played a role in governing his local Episcopal Church; in terms of belief he was inclined toward Deism and the moral philosophy of Christianity.

In a private letter to Benjamin Rush, Jefferson refers to himself as "Christian" (1803): "To the corruptions of Christianity I am, indeed, opposed; but not to the genuine precepts of Jesus himself. I am a Christian, in the only sense in which he wished any one to be; sincerely attached to his doctrines, in preference to all others; ascribing to himself every human excellence..." In a letter to his close friend William Short Jefferson clarified, "it is not to be understood that I am with him [Jesus] in all his doctrines. I am a Materialist; he takes the side of Spiritualism; he preaches the efficacy of repentance toward forgiveness of sin; I require a counterpoise of good works to redeem it. Among the sayings and discourses imputed to him by his biographers, I find many passages of fine imagination, correct morality, and of the most lovely benevolence; and others, again, of so much ignorance, of so much absurdity, so much untruth and imposture, as to pronounce it impossible that such contradictions should have proceeded from the same being."

Jefferson praised the morality of Jesus and edited a compilation of his teachings, omitting the miracles and supernatural elements of the biblical account, titling it "The Life and Morals of Jesus of Nazareth". Jefferson was firmly anticlerical saying that in "every country and every age, the priest has been hostile to liberty. He is always in alliance with the despot...they have perverted the purest religion ever preached to man into mystery and jargon, unintelligible to all mankind, and therefore the safer for their purposes."

Jefferson rejected the idea of immaterial beings and considered the idea of an immaterial Creator a heresy introduced into Christianity. In a letter to John Adams, Jefferson wrote that to "talk of immaterial existences is to talk of nothing. . . .

At what age of the Christian church this heresy of immaterialism, this masked atheism, crept in, I do not know. But a heresy it certainly is. Jesus taught nothing of it. He told us indeed that 'God is a spirit,' but he has not defined what a spirit is, nor said that it is not matter. And the ancient fathers generally, if not universally, held it to be matter: light and thin indeed, an ethereal gas; but still matter."

Wikipedia

I do have my biases and because I am an American I am willing to speak and point out the trends that I do not agree with in the United States today. Since the year 2000, especially after 9-11, the U.S. has become more polarized than ever before. 2000 to 2020 may be a period that is written about in another 40 years if we are still around and have not taken war and other means of making a point to another level based on the lack of communication and reasoning. This is the era that molded my thinking and how I see the world.

What is happening now is doing the same to the youth in their '20s and '30s today. They will become the leaders of tomorrow. We can all learn from history and try to avoid making the same mistakes over and over again. The world is becoming smaller all the time and we cannot survive with old thinking and reasoning. Our way is not the only way. It is only our way. Travel, see other cultures and get the best education you can. Stupidity cost too much and close mindedness is madness at best.

John Lennon said it in simple words and his quote will always be the voice of the '60s for those of us who choose to remember.

Give Peace a Chance

Index

Acknowledgements

I would like to thank a few people who took the time to help proofread "The '60s". I enjoy writing but finding all the grammar mistakes and words needing corrections is a job that I do not look forward to doing. Margaret, Bill and Becky did a good job. Even though they may have had different experiences during this time in their lives they did not try to redirect any of my observations.

I have met interesting people here in Mexico and these three are just an example of the retired talent living here.

ABOUT THE AUTHOR

In the '60s I was surviving the high school experience and living the college life style at UCSB. As all the different events in the U.S. were happening I was struggling to find out who I was, what I believed in and what I wanted to see for the future of America. The '60s molded my thinking and forced me to see things from outside the box. I did not follow the beliefs of the status quo.

My fraternity in college followed the racists founders from the south. I pulled away and joined the ranks of the student body population that saw people of color as equal. A pinched nerve in my back gave me a deferment for the army. I soon joined the ranks of people who did not believe that war was the answer to the world's problems and I even went on a few protest marches.

When Kennedy was assassinated in 1963 and the government came up with a single shooter theory, I did not believe their answer. Many Americans saw the event as a cover-up from the truth. I joined these people who started to question what government was telling us. The "man behind the curtain" quote does come from the Wizard of Oz and represents those people who control aspects of media and try to control how the country thinks. I never followed or believed in whoever was in power without questioning them. "Question Everything" became my motto for the '60s and in the years that followed.

I know that some people who read this book will not agree with my observations and interpretations of the '60s. How I lived during this period help direct me to where I am in my life today. I left the country for nine years from 1970 to 1979 and traveled around the world. (Living Beneath the Radar) I saw the protests against the war becoming more violent and I wanted no part of this direction.

In India I attended meditation courses and have been practicing Vipassana meditation for almost forty years now. I found a spiritual practice that works for my life style. I no longer smoke or drink anything that alters my mental perceptions.

I am not stating any of this to try and influence the reader. We all have our own path. I came across an inspirational quote from a spiritual leader, which states;

"Just because someone is on a different path than your own does not make him right or wrong. He or she is just on a different path."

I spent many years involved in Science of Mind, which is a metaphysical practice to changing one's self. I was a spiritual practioner for twelve years and helped my wife lead a church for three years in Flagstaff, AZ.

I now live in Baja California in Mexico near a small fishing village called San Felipe. My wife and I have been here since 2011 and we are finding our place in this third world country. I have written three books since being here and have started my fourth. "Between a Rock and a Blood Clot" The other books, "Centavo" and "Learning to Love the Peso" and "Living Beneath the Radar" can be found on www.JeffreyRCrimmel.com.

I retired from teaching in 2010. I lived in Flagstaff, Arizona for ten years and in Phoenix, Arizona for a year before making the move to Mexico. I taught special education for twenty-five year in California and Arizona. After moving to Mexico I think I found the answer to a question I have had for many years. What happens to all the special education kids after they grow up. My answer; "They move to Mexico."

Those who did not fit the mold of the school system in the states and are looking for a different life-style that fits their needs seem to have found it in Baja and other towns throughout this country to the south of the U.S. The comparison of the gringo population to special education kids is a joke so any Baja readers need not take the statement seriously. You are fine just the way you are.

We all have events in our lives that influence us to be who we are. Our challenge in life seems to be one of staying on our own course and acknowledging others who are on theirs. There are going to be differences but we have to share the same space (earth) so we need to do so without hurting each other.

Keep doing what you were directed to do in this life and strive to find your happiness in what you do. Bobby McFerrin said it best.

"Don't worry. Be Happy"

Robert "Bobby" McFerrin, Jr. (born March 11, 1950) is a versatile American vocalist and conductor. He is best known for his 1988 hit song "Don't Worry, Be Happy". He is a ten-time Grammy Award winner. He is well known for his unique vocal techniques and singing styles.
Wikipedia

Fin

Work Cited

All references were from **Wikipedia.** All the pictures as well came from their site.

Two references came **Living Beneath the Radar.**

.

www.ingramcontent.com/pod-product-compliance
Lightning Source LLC
Chambersburg PA
CBHW051812090426
42736CB00011B/1439